SOJOURNER METAMORPHOSIS
(URBAN NOMAD)

POETIC COLLECTION OF EXPERIENCES AND THOUGHTS WITH SHORT STORIES (HAPPY NEW YEAR AND OTHERS - ABUJA LITERARY AND ARTS FESTIVAL SHORT STORY ENTRANT 2022) AND WISE SAYINGS

STEPHEN O.I ORUKPE ESQ

BlueRose ONE
Stories Matter
NewDelhi • London

BLUEROSE PUBLISHERS
India | U.K.

Copyright © STEPHEN O.I. ORUKPE ESQ 2024

All rights reserved by author. No part of this publication may be reproduced, stored in a retrieval system or transmitted in any form or by any means, electronic, mechanical, photocopying, recording or otherwise, without the prior permission of the author. Although every precaution has been taken to verify the accuracy of the information contained herein, the publisher assume no responsibility for any errors or omissions. No liability is assumed for damages that may result from the use of information contained within.

BlueRose Publishers takes no responsibility for any damages, losses, or liabilities that may arise from the use or misuse of the information, products, or services provided in this publication.

For permissions requests or inquiries regarding this publication, please contact:

BLUEROSE PUBLISHERS
www.BlueRoseONE.com
info@bluerosepublishers.com
+91 8882 898 898
+4407342408967

ISBN: 978-978-995-496-4

Cover design: Tahira

First Edition: August 2024

SOJOURNER METAMORPHOSIS

DEDICATION

This book is dedicated to my mother, Madam Esther Ailuelo Orukpe whose support over the years has assisted in no small measure to ensure the completion of this work and other books published.

To my wife Mrs. Rita Esokhanfo Orukpe and brothers Gideon and Israel Orukpe for their support.

God continue to bless you all.

I am deeply grateful.

PREFACE

I discovered poetry in 1996 and since then have penned my thoughts, emotions and feelings, amounting now to over one hundred (112) poems to my credit and still counting.

Overtime, I further discovered short stories and have written quite a few (FIVE actually) in these past years. One of the short stories "HAPPY NEW YEAR", a fictional representation of growing up and actually to re- write the misrepresentation of a thirteen year old as depicted by Chimamanda Adiche in her book "Half A Yellow Sun" in honour of the words of late Chinue Achebe who said those who are unhappy with his book "There Was A Country", should feel free to write theirs. I was unhappy with that misrepresentation and decided to write mine to balance the equation.

Among the things that has kept me going is motivational or wise sayings. I love quotes especially of great men and women and has led me to my penning down also wise sayings from my experiences and that of others.

This book is a three band cord that cannot be broken. It comprises of my poems, short stories and my wise sayings as well as that of others.

My gift and contribution to the world and humanity.

Stephen Orukpe Esq.

TABLE OF CONTENT

Dedication ---ii
Preface ---iii
Table of Content --iv

Short Story (1)

ALL IN GOD's NAME ---1

POEMS

(1) RUDE AWAKENING --9

SUCCESS NUGGET ---10
Three Things That Kills Dreams -----------------------------------10

POEMS
    (2) A WRITER's DILENMA --------------------------------------11
    (3) WHIRLWIND ---13
    (4) FLAME --14
    (5) SLAUGHTER HOUSE ---15
    (6) CHINA WARE --17
    (7) CLOUD OF JOY --17
    (8) THOUGHTS --17
    (9) GONE WITH THE WIND -----------------------------------18
    (10) THE ORIGINAL --19
    (11) UNBROKEN CHAIN ---------------------------------------20
    (12) ANGER ---20
    (13) MISSED --21

(14) PRISONER --- 21
(15) CAN ONLY SOAR HIGH ------------------------------ 21
(16) LOST LOVE --- 22
(17) EVERYDAY -- 23
(18) WAY BACK -- 23
(19) OBUKO -- 24
(20) MOLUE -- 25
(21) BEING HIGH -- 26
(22) BEAUTIFUL NONSENSE ---------------------------- 27
(23) MONDAY --- 28
(24) TIME TO HUNT THE HUNTER ---------------------- 29

SHORT STORY (2)
CAUGHT A NEW DAWN --------------------------------- 30

POEMS
(25) RAINFALL --- 39
(26) UNBELIEVABLY TRUE ------------------------------ 39
(27) REMEMBER -- 40
(28) UNBELIEVABLY TRUE ------------------------------ 42
(29) REMEMBER -- 44
(30) MY HOME -- 46
(31) ACHABA SPLENDOUR ------------------------------ 46
(32) RISING -- 47
(33) LEVEL --- 48
(34) MYSTERY LADY ------------------------------------- 49
(35) I FEEL LIKE --- 49
(36) HOW I FEEL -- 50
(37) SUFFER --- 50
(38) ONE TURN --- 51
(39) MEH UNA NO VEX ---------------------------------- 51
(40) LET HER KNOW ------------------------------------- 52

v

(41) LOOKING AT HER ------------------------------------- 53
(42) STATIC --53
(43) ARISE|BE UNIFIED -------------------------------53
(44) TO BE A MAN -------------------------------------55
(45) THE QUEST SEEKERS --------------------------56
(46) DESPERATE MUGU ----------------------------58
(47) DOMITTILA --58
(48) AFRO WESTERNER ----------------------------59
(49) LET THOSE WITH EARS HEAR ----------------------61
(50) SUCH REMEMBRANCE-------------------------------64
(51) SO ALONE --64
(52) MY LOVE --64
(53) TORTURE CHAMBER----------------------------------65
(54) MY HEART WOULD GO ON ------------------------65
(55) CROSS ROAD --65
(56) KNOWING WHO -------------------------------------66
(57) IF ONLY ---67

SHORT STORY (3)
WHAT GOES AROUND, COMES AROUND --------------67

  POEMS
(58) FLASHBACK ---76
(59) TAILGATE FOR DEAR LIFE ----------------------------77
(60) GOD SAVE THE DEAD --------------------------------78
(61) BELOVED --79
(62) THIS SOMETHING ----------------------------------80
(63) REAPER --81
(64) LUST ---81
(65) BLOOMING FLOWER ---------------------------------82
(66) NOTHING BUT DREAMS -----------------------------82

vi

(67) FEBRUARY 28 --84
(68) DRUNKEN SOUL --------------------------------------85
(69) BLACK QUEEN MOTHER ---------------------------87
(70) MY FLOWER --88
(71) HIS MOST HIGH ---------------------------------------89
(72) HIS REFLECTION --------------------------------------90
(73) LOVE --92
(74) NO TIME IS LATE -------------------------------------93
(75) THINKING OF YOU -----------------------------------95
(76) VISION --96
(77) WELCOME BACK --------------------------------------98
(78) SOOTHING BALM -------------------------------------99
(79) NAUGHTY ---100
(80) IN HIS PRESENCE -----------------------------------100
(81) JUST AWESOME --------------------------------------100

SHORT STORY (4)
CUNNY MAN DIE, CUNNY MAN BURY AM ---------------101

(82) WE FELL APART --------------------------------------108
(83) RAINFALL --109
(84) FUNK --110
(85) JUST YOU --110
(87) JUST THINKING --------------------------------------111
(88) FRIEND ---111
(89) CYCLE --121
(90) BLACK MEMORIAM ----------------------------------121
(91) BROKEN DAWN --------------------------------------122

WISDOM NUGGETS

POEMS ---123

(92) THIS TIME --124
(93) CIRCLE --124
(94) BLACK CYCLE --126
(95) THE RUNWAY ---125
(96) SMILE ---126
(97) GODDESS --127
(98) HOPE --127
(99) RESOLUTION ---128
(100) NOT AFRAID --128
(101) WELCOME --130

196 WISE SAYINGS OF MINE AND OTHERS ----------------131

POEMS
(101) SOLDIER OF THE LAW --------------------------------150
(102) TONGUES OF DIFFERENCE ---------------------------151
(103) GREATER TOMORROW -------------------------------152
(104) WEDDING THINGS---154
(105) THONG THINGS --157
(106) IF I BE A POET THAT ---------------------------------------170
(107) SING MY SONG NOW --------------------------------------171
(108) WETIN DEY INSIDE SEF ------------------------------------172
(109) NO COMPETITION --174
(110) POETRY IS......---175
(111) BATTLEGROUND NDA --------------------------------------175
(112) LETTING LOOSE ---176

ALL IN GOD'S NAME

One beautiful Sunday after church proceedings when people are found shattered around.
'Hello, Sister Martha, greeted a man.
Turning around
'Oh, good afternoon, Pastor James', replied Martha
'How was the service today?
'It was splendid, I really felt the presence of the Holy-Ghost right in this place and Pastor James, your sermon, was really inspiring'
'Let's give God the glory, I also was highly lifted by your special number, it made me see the glory of God come down'
'God be praised, who can do all things through his Son Jesus Christ'.
'Sister Martha, I won't be staying long like you might have heard me say earlier on but I wouldn't want to miss the golden opportunity of meeting a highly exulted sister in Christ'
'And who might that be? Asked Sister Martha
'It's you of course'
'Me', quiet surprised.
'Yes you, through out my ministerial journey around the world, I haven't met a more glorified, highly exulted and beautiful songstress as you and please pardon my indulgence'
'No not at all, God be praised, but I don't think am any of these compliment you said'.
Sister Martha, somebody called.
Answering and afterwards excusing herself to go attend to the caller.
'I would be waiting for your return', he said.
'I don't think I would be long'. Taking her leave.
'Hello Pastor James', someone cuts in

'Hi Sis....ter'
'Grace', she answered.
'Yes, Sister Grace, bless you'
'We are having our singles and youth meeting and it's time already, Sister Martha is the secretary' she explained.
'That's nice, let me see the Pastor'. Taking his leave.

Pastor James was visiting the church for the first time, he had known the Pastor-in-charge for quite sometime before they lost contact. It was in some pastors conference that both met again and he was invited to the next Sunday worship by the pastor-in-charge as a guest.
On the said Sunday, after welcoming of visitors, Pastor James was introduced formally by the pastor-in-charge. Although he earlier had hinted to his congregation about having an important visitor in their midst.
'I want to introduce someone whom, I had lost contact with for quiet sometime but dramatically we met, let me introduce to you Pastor James' announced the Pastor-In-Charge.
Everyone in the congregation stood and applauded for the man of God as he stepped to the altar to shake and embrace the Pastor-In-Charge.
'I believe you have a word or two for the congregation' asked the Pastor-In-Charge as he handed over the microphone to his guest.
'Praise the Lord', Pastor James shouted into the microphone.
'Alleluia', everybody answered.
'It is true, we have known each other for quite sometime before losing contact, really, all this while, I've been on what is known as mobile ministration, moving from here to there and I've been fortunate to have ministered in countries like Canada, South-Africa, Botswana, Kenya,

Britain, The United States Of America, Ghana, Senegal and a host of other countries.'
' I only just, recently returned from Senegal where am helping to build a church, as I am standing here, the holy spirit just ministered in my spirit this words "Dry bones shall rise again".
'Repeat after me, dry bones shall rise again,' he shouted.
'Dry bones shall rise again', everyone shouted
'Just believe it, dry bones shall rise again, in your business'.
'Amen', chorused everyone.
'In your marriages'.
'Amen'.
'In your family'.
'Amen'.
'At your place of work'.
'Amen'
'In your going out and in your coming in'.
'Amen'.
'In your every work of life. I see it, I see it; in this church'.
'Aaaaaaaaaameeen! Everyone thundered with an applause.
'Somebody shout alleluia.
'Alleluia'.
'Ooooooh, I feel it somebody!
'Yes', shouted everyone
'You know, during ministration as such, the keyboard ought to be sending some soul inspiring tunes, but I can see that there isn't one around, for this am going to provide the church with a key-board'. He said.
At this point, everybody stood on their feet, shouts of praise the lord rented the air.
Handing the microphone back to the Pastor-in-Charge, he stepped down from the pulpit to his reserved seat in front.
'We give God the glory, for that exulted ministration. I hope

a lot of you might be challenged as to coming forward to do something for God', explained the Pastor-in-Charge.

Before the service came to an end, Pastor James had already sighted a lady, he felt was right for him; after service, when all formalities where over, he calculated his time and proceeded to finish a work.

'Ah, you are back! Pastor James exclaimed.
'I want to be going home', sister Martha explained.
'Where do you live? He inquired.
'Three streets from here, at the ECOMOG quarters! She replied.
'Then we are practically heading in the same direction, for I am putting up with a friend at oil resources quarters, shall we then'.
'Sure'.
'But please, let me quickly, say goodbye to the pastor'. He said.
'No problem'. She quickly puts in.
On their way home.
'Sister Martha, please, let me apologise, my car is in Senegal.
'Oh, I understand'.
'So sister Martha, tell me a little about yourself'. He asked.
'Well, there is nothing really about me, I work with the ECOMOG in the library section as head librarian'.
'And you say, there is nothing. Sister, learn to keep on thanking God, no matter, how little'. He explained.
'Are you engaged for marriage?
'No, why are you asking'. She puts in.
'I was just, a little inquisitive, you know, I see God using you greatly especially in the music ministry, have you ever for once, thought of it? He asked.
'No, not at all'. She said.
'Anyway, I think, it is worth mentioning to your pastor'.

'It would be nice, but I don't think am ready yet'.
'What do you mean by not been ready yet, a lot of us, where called into ministry, when the going was really good but as the bible says, one has to forsake is father, mother, everything, pick up his cross and follow him'. He explained. 'So my sister, always be ready and also keep praying about it'.
'I will'.

It is now three weeks now and pastor James didn't go as planned, all this while, he was always around sister Martha, visiting her at home, staying late at her place, escorting her after each service, encouraging her with the message of the gospel. However, he was yet to fulfil his pledge to the church concerning the keyboard.
'Sister Martha', called the pastor-in-charge after service on the forth Sunday.
'Yes Pastor'. She answered.
He continued, 'I called you here to really, find out, what is the matter?
'I don't understand, sir'. She replied, looking lost.
'What I mean your relationship with Pastor James'. He inquired.
'Oh, that, there is nothing between us, other than the friendship of the body of Christ'. She explained.
'But the way you two are going, it troubles me in the spirit, I feel something isn't right but I can't figure out what it is. You see truly I know Pastor James but that was a long time, right now, I can say nothing really about him and his faith is questionable'. He puts in.
'I've heard what you said, Pastor, I would be careful'. She answered.
'Goodbye Sister Martha'.
'Goodbye Pastor'.

'I will continue praying for you'.
During the evening of the same day at sister Martha's house, Pastor James came around as usual on a visit.
'Good evening Pastor'.
'Good evening Sister Martha, I can see the glory of God radiating around you and shining on you, making you as beautiful as you can ever be.'
'Haba, Pastor!, She answered blushing.
'I mean it, only you cannot borrow my eyes, you then might see and thus believe. He explained.
'Pastor, you sef! Abeg leave me jare'. She said feeling impressed by his comment.
' Look here Sister Martha, I believe the Lord is calling the both of us to become one', settling himself properly.
'What are you trying to imply'.
'It is simple, the Lord has put it in my heart right from the beginning, that you are the one I would settle down with, am saying will you marry me?
Feeling confused and not finding words, Sister Martha was jostled out of her slumber into reality.
'You are proposing to me right? She asked.
' That's exactly what am doing' he replied.
'But I don't really know you'.
'Does it matter, anyway I want to travel down to Lagos in a week's time, tell me will you marry me?.
'Let me pray over it, before answering'. She answered.
Moving closer to her and holding her hands.
'Look here, Sister Martha, look at me, right from the first time I saw you, the Lord told me, that is your woman, in whom am well pleased'.
Holding her hands even closer and moving really close, he kissed her, caressing her face.
'What are you trying to do Pastor James?'
'Relax, Sister Martha, I am but showing you the conviction

needed to prove that we are destined for each other'.
'But the bible says, a thing as this is an act of fornication, which is a sin'. She tried to explain, while showing signs of shyness.
'Don't you know the bible alo said that to the pure, all things are pure and it is not good for a man to be alone, he must seek out his bride and the two shall become one'.
At this stage, he was really massaging her, touching her sensitive parts, foundling her breasts, kissing her lips and was only slowed down by the weak protest of Sister Martha. Capitalizing on this sign of weakness, slowly, gently and soundlessly, they both came and became one.
After some few weeks!
'Pastor James, I've missed my period'. Explained Sister Martha
'Since when did you notice it? Asked Pastor James
'Two weeks now, you met me at my peak period and you were not protected'.
'It is no problem, as I have said earlier, am going to marry you'.
'Then we have to get married before the pregnancy starts to show'. She said, looking worried.
'In that case, I have to go to Lagos to inform my people, but as you know, I don't have a kobo, all the money am expecting hasn't come'.
'Like how much would you need?' She asked.
'About seven hundred thousand naira'.
'But that is too much'.
'I know but it's only a loan, I have a reputation to preserve and it will help me fasten the money am expecting and prepare for a grand wedding with you'.
'Ok, but all I can afford is five hundred thousand naira and its all the money I have in my savings'.
'Good, bring it, that can do something', he said adding

'Darling, I won't make you regret this, if not that the money am expecting hasn't arrive, why should I collect money from you, after all this I would take you to Senegal where all my assets are, from there we could relocate to the States or any European country of your choice and continue our ministry'. Kissing her fore head.

It is now two months since Pastor James left for Lagos, Sister Martha is already getting agitated and worry sign's is beginning to show.
'What would I do now, I would wait a little longer, he would come back soon. Oh God please, let him come back soon and in safety'. She prayed, while speaking to herself.
A knock on the door brought her to consciousness.
'The door is open', she said.
'Sister Martha, what is wrong with you?' inquired her visitor.
'Ha, Sister Grace, you are back from Makurdi, how was your trip? Three months seem like yesterday?'.
'It was very fine, how are things around here?'
'Everything is fine'.
'But you don't look fine', she replied, and 'if I may ask, where is Pastor James?'
'Em, he travelled to Lagos!'
'Travelled? Look Sister, I have hot ist for you, do you know that all the testimonies of Pastor James are very rotten and false, all those talk about Europe, Asia, Africa, South-Continental are all but lies.
'Tell me something'.
'Do you know that all this while he had been at Otukpo doing his ministerial job before indulging in fornication with a lady in the church, promising to marry her afterwards, before he was expelled; whereas he already had a wife and two kids'.

At this instance, Sister Martha jumped up on her feet.
'Ah, my pregnancy, my money, my life, oh am finished'.
Speaking absent-mindedely
'What's all this you are saying? Inquired Sister Grace, looking confused.
......Collapsing.....
'Ah, Ah, Sister Martha, Jesus, Jesus, somebody help me, anybody, ah, he has ruined her.'

(1)
RUDE AWAKENING

I was jostled from my
Sleep, to the harsh reality
Of my being
Awakened!
Ah, so I sleep
All along, I sleep
Daydreaming in the wanton
Of my being.
Overshadowed with the
Sordid aura of supposed reality.
I shuddered
On realization day
Realizing my indepth folly of meanings.
Of understanding
For so awakened
To the realized
Conditionality of my mortality.
Embroided with un-certainty
For certainty
I stand affirm
On realization day
As I yearn awake in my awakenedness.

SUCCESS NUGGET
THREE THINGS THAT KILL DREAMS

(1) Despair- always find something doing, never let worry crip into your life. There is so much out there to do; people to meet; opportunities to grab. So never you let yourself be despaired by anything, know that all are shadow and dust. What you say reality is, is what it is and nothing more.

(2) Discouragement – never be discouraged, even if you have done a particular task over and over again. At all times be with your complete faculty of reason. Your power lies in your thinking. If no one encourages you, endeavor to always encourage yourself.

(3) Doubt- never have doubt and if you are to have it, let it serve as the oil for your machinery for action to achieve that which you set out to accomplish.

IT IS GLORIOUS TO BE SUCCESSFUL AND AT THE APPOINTED TIME THIS SON OF MAN SHALL BE MADE MANIFEST. FOR NOTHING IS IMPOSSIBLE. IT IS ONLY TIME.
Never have regrets, always take your opportunity and never regret; see the future and act on it.
Repetition calls for lasting and deeper impression, so dominate that situation.

(2)
A WRITER'S DILENMA

I feel so eluded
Dumbstrucked   imprisoned
By my intel   lock with no luck
to unpluck
this dangling
this swinging
this hanging
see it, feel it, touch it, have it.
Nooo,
Scared to envelop
In the warm embrace of my
Cuddle.
Afraid to be brought alive,
Created for immortality;
She is shy
Soothe her
Get her pampered
Anoint with H_2O,
Please come my dear
As visualized
As conceptualized
As realized.
Place it
Where
Were
The trash is sheets compatriots.

ii

Words elude me

I cannot seem to feel it
Oh, see it
There it is now, come
Do not be shy
Come fill my papyrus
Spill your guts:
For immortality reborn after
Series in incubation.
My labour is so painful,
Lying in labour room
For word birth
Perfect
Non-perfect
Match
Rematch
Mis-match
Not match.
Am at my tethers
Ready to explode
Raving like an infection of affliction
Mesmerized among sheets of shits
Placing square pegs
In round holes
Clipped for un-clipping
Fitting rightly
Not wrongly
In this illusion
Of creation
For eternity.
The trash is sheets comrade

(3)
WHIRLWIND

It feels like peace
Soothely deserving
Of a nymph.
A train is coming
A caravan of gypsies
Trailing a monotone
Of monosyllable.
Hear
    Listen,
That eve's daughter
Vocal cords,
Refreshing, reassuring
Resembling, resonating
Of monassembling
One track sound
Of a one way train
Actificial special on bell's piece.
Call the traffic warders
Prepare the traffic lighters
For the vocal lybarinths
Pirators
Are come to town.

(4)
FLAME

Encroached in that dark alley
Cut from view behind that stall
Two lovers, entangled in
Their love affair
Engrossed in that
Minute ecstasy
But I heard
Smoke lovers ……….. young

Oh, shut up
Pervert mouth
Of a demented mind
I've heard it before
Today, it is not
Yesterday it was not
Tomorrow it would not
That smaoke lovers…… young

Give me some more
Fill me up
Dislodge the law of equilibrium
Ah, one cannot beat that
But this cancer stick
Would.
A day is not made without
Consensus ad idem with
This minute lover of
Refreshxation.
Though smoke lovers………young

Liable
Who is liable
Are you liable?
Am inured
Immunized
Helping the economy
Increase its VAT production.
I would sue
That umbrage
On a gentlemind
Of smoke lovers..... young.

Going where
Am right here
Always refreshed after meeting
With my flame mistress.
Be not deceived
What is wrong
Is not right.
Discriminatory use would make
Smoke lovers.... Young

(5)
SLAUGHTER HOUSE

Guided towards the gallow
A willingness of accepted fate
Stripping voluntarily….
Out spread…..
With suppressed cry,
Soft muted sobs of joy
From pangs of defloration
Flinching not, wringling on.
Exhaustive slumber, later on.

iii

Complete and delicious
Leading to slake all
Pent-up longings
Upon the warmth
Of an eager flesh.
To be drawn
From appeasement, later on
Into dreamless sleep.

(6) CHINA WARE

Hold her gently
Carry her with care
My Dresden china
Lest she breaks.

(7) CLOUD OF JOY

How strange
How sweet,
This gift of love.
Such a generous gift.
Not lust of flesh
Not urgent communion
Of one yearning shove
For love.
But, true love
That transcends time
Itself; having no barriers
In class
In race
In creed
In country.

(8) THOUGHTS

I fear you
      Master of illusion
Creator of creation
      Marker of imperfect
Turn perfect

      Like atlantis of completeness
Making the unbelievable
      Turn believable
In a real fantasy
      To be crushed
And crashed
      By weaker-minded
Mortals.

(9)
GONE WITH THE WIND

You are gone with the wind
Blown all over far, faraway
Sailed with the wind
Forever with time.
When would we ever meet?
My heart goes out to you
Wherever you are.

No more chattering-clattering
Shopping to impress on resumption
Gone are hand shakes
And faces beaming with smiles
Bringing with you newer tales.

Oh, gone with the wind
Would I ever see you again?
Old times sure don't come back
What would I do now?
With you always on my mind.

Let me be blown
By the wind, to be

Where you are, forever.
Tasting of your sweet honey
Never tired of having
Enough of your ripen grapes
Clamouring for more.

The wind blows
At everyone looking haggard
At lastdays, planless
Without nothing
But managing
To go on.

(10)
THE ORIGINAL

My original
    Lit a fire
      Down at
        The inner
          Most
      Holy
        Of
          Holies.
Setting a consuming fire
   An overwhelming desire
      At the root of this base
             Matter.
Upturned foolish wisdom
     Created a blank
        Insatiable thirsting
          But spurned quenching
Only now quenched
  By THE original.

(11)
UNBROKEN CHAINS

I see
    Tomorrow never dies
As my today fades
Away.
Tears unshed
Wells upon my bowel sack
Waiting turns to march
Down the silvery hill.
I see
Tomorrow never dies.

(12)
ANGER

Hold it
 Press it
  Down.
Biting
 Anguishing   ly.
The poison
   Gradually
    Rising
      Smoldering
       Antagonizing
      Choking
       Seeking
     A
       Chanel
      To
        Let
         Go.

(13)
MISSED

I came a wooing
And left a booing
So much a losing
This heart a fooling

(14)
PRISONER

As an hostage
I cannot think of what
To think to say.
As an hostage
In my supposed home
A so called fatherland.
As an hostage
Not knowing what to do
Not knowing what not to do.
As am used continually like a tool
By the despicable duel
Between ASUU and federal government.
As an hostage
Yes am angry
But not hungry
Though I hunger
For my life
To once again
Be as I say it should be.

(15)
CAN ONLY SOAR HIGH

Though it would take me time
I would conquer and rise high above poverty.

Though it would take me time
I would conquer and rise above lack.
Though it will take me time
I would attain a high level of intelligence.
Though it would take me time
I would attain a high level of understanding.
Though it will take me time
I would attain a high level of retentiveness.
Though it would take me time
I would attain sound knowledge.
Though it will take me time
I would maintain strength.
Though it would take me time
I would attain wisdom.
Though it would take me time
I would increase in integrity.

(16)
LOST LOVE

Frustrating love becomes
Prowling along, pocket empty.
Forced show of thirty-two

Such happiness, never found
Such freedom never discovered
No presupposition on the weight of
Ones pocket.
I am not selfish; I am quite truthful.
I have no diamonds
I have no gold
I have no precious-stone
I have no persian notes.
Yet, to love is to give
And not to give is not to love.

Make me a giver to love
And not have to give
In this age of pocket-love.

(17)
EVERYDAY

Everyday…….
Seems like the other day
Unnoticedly dull, uneventfully hopeless.
Everyday……
I have no use for time
Moreless its happenings.
Everyday………….
Unfolding of a new chapter
From the events for continuity
The scenes of nothingness.
Oh! Would time be my redeemer?
A light in my path of darkness?
Would my wheel turn around?
I don't know, for it looks useless
Uneventfully hopeless.
Everyday, like all other days.

(18)
WAYBACK

So very long
It seems to be
All forgotten but not faded out
Seeing you again
Evolved in glad tidings
Bringing it all back
Like as if it was yesterday.

(19)
OBUKO (1)

That's what you really are
Haba sef(2), yours is truly much
Your batteryless torch-light
Charges to full anytime
It spots a beautiful figure eight
Making your nepa pole suffer
Un necessarily.

You are never tired
After all the booting
All the snobbing, plus insults
You are but still running
After the skirt.
She no want to give you chop(3)
Abi(4) you no dey(5) hear
Or is it understanding you lack?

You have chased
With all goodies
E no(6) still succumb
Northwardly
Southwardly
You have followed
Still you no get am(7).

Obuko(8) who smells after
Crying to be giving to eat
Running up and down
Right and left
Climbing, falling, a continuous

Failing succession but still
Hoping to eat,
That's what you are
OBUKOOOOoooo……(9)

   (1) He goat (2)exclamation (3) eat (4) or (5) are (6)she
   (7) didn't (8) he goat

(20)
MOLUE (1)

King of Lagos roads
Backbone of the economy
Defenders of lagosians movement
You who have no substitute.
Can the danfo's(2) contest with you?
What of the keke-marwa's(3)?
Or is it the achaba's(4)?
Molue, formidable as you are
Contesting for supremacy
Like a vexed lion
Charging as if would crash
But only scratching.
Even though you lack courtesy
You are still loved by many.
Never belly-filled(5), always wanting more.
Packing humans like sardines
Your pilot always has to be
In line with your morale
Never satisfied, continuous
Oliver twisting.
Shouts of bus stops, duro' o'(6)
Onwole' o'(7), mu' chagi' e' ja de'(8)
Owa', arugbo' ni'(9), o' kpo' omo' o'(10)

Continuous thrilling thearteric.
Molue! Oh Molue!
The cross, the moon and star
Medichanting
Have found a comfortable
Abode, as no day passes without
Refreshment.
Your stewards can never collect
Complete fare, continuous I be
Staff, son' owo' mi' kpe'(12)
Collect money for front
Abi na(13)back or centre?
All rants by a toothless bulldog.
Molue, what would lagos be without you?
How would Lagos look without you/
Molue, who wants to contest with you
Let him first conquer is
Age group.
Savior of the Lagos masses
You who made Lagos what it is
Let my praise reach you.

(1) Lagos State public transport (2)mini transport buses (3)tricycles (4)motorcycles (5)never satisfied (6) stop (7) getting in (8)prepare your fares with change (9)stop (10) an elderly person (11) she is backing a child (12) pay my complete fare

(21)
BEING HIGH

When I am high

I careless for all around me
Feeling on top of the world.
Nothing matters, all worries a past-time
All hopes accomplished in time.
Remaining unmoved with the world
Tumbling down around me.
Nothing quite matters
Floating in my world
Higher and higher you float
Deeper and deeper you go
Becoming more and more wiser.
Just like a car
Refilled with fuel
Bouncing back to life.
To conquer the miles
Regardless of no Goliath.
Clear, I say clear
Before I squach you under my squelching tar.

(22)
BEAUTIFUL NONSENSE

That is what life is
 A Beautiful nonsense
The entry into the world
But a delirious struggle
A struggle for survival
A struggle for co-existence
Growing up a struggle
A struggle for recognition
A struggle for the basics of life
A struggle to keep whats ones
At the tail end a struggle to depart.
Tell me what is not a struggle in life's elaborate annals?
What is the use of multiplying

To be led astray
Then judged and led finally
Into sulphur in conjuction with brimstone
A struggle for salvation
A struggle from temptation
A struggle to enter into
Forever lightness, no hunger, no thirst
But a continuous struggle
Of assemblic worship.
Oh! Life in general is but a
Heap of beautiful nonsense.

(23)
MONDAY

After a long day rest
Being the first on the row
The creator spent time on your making
As the heavenly maids surrounded your being
You were given the skin of melted gold
Radiatingly smooth.
You were given hairs weaved out from
Rich Persian wools
Dyed in the trench hold of the altar.
You were given eyes made of sapphire
So clear like the skies.
You were given lips crested with ruby.
You were formed from onyx
And given breast, so full and soft.
You were endowed with a backyard
An eight wonder, your weapon on
Unguarded obukos(1).
Your creation took the specialty
Of Diana herself.
To make meaning of this beautiful nonsense.

And the creator was satisfied
With your creation.
A man who does not look
At you twice
Is not a man.
A man who turns
Not his head twice
Is but a walking dead.
Oh! Beautiful! Enchantingly beautiful!
Forever I would be by your side
Washing your velvety shaped legs with
My kisses.
For indeed you were
But created on a Monday.

   (1) He goat

(24)
TIME TO HUNT THE HUNTER

Mosquitoes! Oh mosquitoes!
What have I done?
Tell me, what have I done?
To be dealt with like this.

Striking under night cover
Whim, whim, here and there
Disturbing sweet dreams
Compounded with blackout.

White man's concoction
Seems an added advantage
To streaming lineages
Forming them antibodies.

I cease to be
Seeming to be the hunted
No more relaxing, but
Hitting back where stopped.

I cannot sit with hands
At akimbo, hoping to
Enjoy sweet dreams
With lingering mosquitoes.

I the hunted
Hunts the hunter
Lessening the disturbance
For the night to come.

Mosquitoes am out for you
Mosquitoes am ready for you
Mosquitoes be prepared
I am very prepared for you.

SHORT STORY (2)

CAUGHT A NEW DAWN

On this particular day, at about 5:30am, democracy has been instituted and a new President elected, I woke up feeling dull and frightened, not really knowing what was wrong. The kind of feeling you have without placing a finger on your mood.

Still trying to get myself, I was woken into full consciousness by my mother's voice.

'jeff, jeff, are you such a kid to be woken up', said my mother, adding 'or have you forgotten you would be

traveling today?.
'I haven't forgotten mum', I replied strecting myself out of the bed.
'Then why are you still on your bed at this time'?
I kept mute
'Why don't you run along and get prepared, you know what a long journey is there before you'.
Mothers! I wouldn't blame her for this early morning scolding, I had two weeks before received my NYSC call up letter and was required to report to camp some weeks after and being in the far north, Maiduguri in Borno State to be precise, I intended to stop over in Abuja and meet my Uncle who resides at Garki to see what I can squeeze out of him.
'Are you still in the bathroom or don't you know what the time is saying', my mum shouted.
'Almost ready', I shouted out of the bathroom.
'If you like don't be ready, spend all the day in there bathing and dressing like you've got all day'.
I rush at my bath, brushed my teeth, did my toileting and then applied my body cream and perfume, as I dressed up very quickly, having already packed the night before and then combing my hair, I went to my mum's room.
'That's fifteen thousand naira, please manage it, you know I don't have much. This is the much I can do', she said.
What would I do but to collect it, luckily, I had an extra five thousand naira, adding to make it twenty thousand naira. I felt kind of big with all the money in my pocket.
'Jeff! Called mum
'You know, what I want from you?
'No mum'
'Continue to hold yourself in integrity and God would continue to florish you in your doings, strengthen you where you go weak, cautioning you when you go wrong and guiding you wherever you thread', She prayed.

'Amen'
'Go in peace'
I left her, went on to my room, grabbed my bags and headed for the park.
'Greet my brothers and sisters when they get back from school on holiday', I said
'Your message would reach them', She said.

Since my Father died, mum had been our father and mother. She didn't remarry, for I believe she either loved him very much or she wanted to make sure we all are trained fully without any complications.
As I entered the bus leading to the park, my mood became pleasant and boisterous, I have always wanted to go on a long journey aboard a marco polo, for I have heard too many interesting stories about this monstrous land plane of styles and comfort. I was tired of boarding the regular sixteen sitter buses and have always paid the price of uncomfortable, saucy drivers and squeezed in passengers.
So I resolved to board this land plane seeing I have enough money on me and knowing also that once I met my uncle, something big is sure.
Arriving at the booking center of long line transport, there was a fairly long queue but all the same I managed to secure my ticket. As I was moving towards the park canteen, something caught my fancy; an angel to be precise was sitting in the middle of a hefty guy and an elderly lady. Looking at her made my heart skip and it seemed out of place for my heart had never skipped before especially when I fancy a lady, all I had always done was just to walk up and introduce myself but this time it was the opposite.
Immediately I got into the restaurant, I brought out my lucky coin, head is always positive while tail is negative, I tossed the coin to know my luck, it landed with the head

showing. I tried again and still the same result, still tried a last time due to my anxiety, feeling as if I was making it seem positive but still the last toss still bounced on the head but later faced the other side due to it fallen at the edge of the table.

'Today, seem's to be a lucky day', I said to myself.

I slotted my coin back into my wallet and gave my order, half way through the meal, an announcement came over the loud speakers beckoning on passengers to board for departure. I rushed at my food, finished my drink, and rushed to the bus, passengers had already started to board, quickly I skimmed the area but did not see her, with the haste I was in, I mistakenly brushed someone.

'Excuse me mister, what's the rush about, is the bus running away/, said the stranger. I quickly apologized, got on the bus and made my way to where my seat number should be, as I made my way into the bus, I was transfigured, for she was sitting directly facing me and her look was so inviting, I just couldn't pass.

'Is anyone here', I asked. 'Not that I know of', she answered. 'Then I better make myself comfortable', sitting down and looking straight but my mind was running wild, what should I say, if the owner of this seat should appear, what would I do. But by providence, nobody accosted me concerning the seat   after the bus started on its way; they keep to time, whether the bus is full or not.

'Are you travelling alone', I finally found my voice to ask.

'Yeah, anything! She replied

'No, not really but I felt I won't be doing myself any good, if I let you waste like that', I said.

'Waste as how? She said with a grin

'Not really waste', beginning to find my voice again, 'what am trying to say is that, I don't think you or I might want this journey to be our last encounter', I said.

'How do you mean, not wanting it to be our last encounter with you? She asked.
So sweetly said but I was not ready to be put off.
'You know what, before I proceed, let me introduce myself, I am Jefferson Omogbiede from Edo State, finished from Federal Polytechnic Auchi and studied mass communication, on my way to Maiduguri for nysc.'
'Oh, well am Zainab, I'm from Kano State and presently in my third year at the university of Lagos studying english'. She replied
'Our courses are related you know', I put in
'Sure sure, If you look at it in a way'
'You know what Zainab, you don't look hausa'
'What', really'
'Maybe because, your uniform isn't on'
'Oh, my head scarf, you mean?
'Yes, yes, you can pass for a southerner'
'Hmmmmmmmm, really, that' good'
'That aside, I don't want this to be our last encounter', I said adding, 'I see this as the beginning of a splendid relationship being planted right now.'
'How do you know, you seem so sure of yourself', She replied.
I looked straight into her eyes for a few second before replying.
'Zainab, I must confess, I haven't felt this way in my whole life, it seem something lost is found,, the first time I set my eyes on you', I said adding, 'and I wouldn't want this opportunity to slip past my being or for a long time would I continue to mourn this moment'.
Her unusual quietness signified her intense attention to what I was saying.
'I must confess, your beauty has no substitute' I began again

'Common stop pulling my legs, I'm not that beautiful'.
'But you are, zainab look at me'.
She shylishly raised her head a little bit.
'Look at me', I said
Raising her head higher and looking directly at me.
'I love you zainab', I said.
'But you don't know me and I also don't know you, so how can you say, you love me, when we are only just meeting for the first time?
My heart skipped a little and my heart beat increased.
'That's the more reason why am confessing my love for you', I heard myself say, adding ' Can't you sense the way am feeling? Really love doesn't ask why, it is about feelings, for it is from the heart' 'Zainab please don't reject my love for you.'
'How am I to trust you', she said adding, 'I don't want to be disappointed, for guys are not to be trusted.'
'Zainab trust me, looking at this from the beginning, you should know that we were destined for each other, don't do something that you would regret later', I said.
'Jeff', she called
'Yes love', I answered
'Promise me, you won't break my heart', she said.
'I promise, as long as I breath, I would continue to love you', I replied.
Her look gave me the required answer and my heart melted with joy. Already a nice movie was showing on the screen- The Titanic- we sat back enjoying the film, using our hands to send messages.
We finally got to lokoja, even though we were served with snacks and soft drinks, some people just want to stop and stretch.
The stop gave us a little freedom and an opportunity to get to know each other better.

'So tell me about yourself,' she asked.
'Well, there is nothing about me really, just that am on my way to answer the clarion call, was born some twenty-five years ago, father dead, mother had been our all and the third in a family of six.'
'So how about you, I asked.
'Well, forth daughter in a family of five, some twenty years old and going home on holiday.'
'Are you stopping over, like me in Abuja or you reside there?' I asked
'I actually reside in Abuja and live around the Asokoro district.'
'Ah you must be amongst the politicians or big business people to be living there.'
'Not at all'.
'Tell me the truth?
'That's why I didn't take a flight, you know people here and there all pointing at you, trying to get you into a conversation', she complained.
'Then you are some sort of celebrity! Hmmmm
'Well am the forth daughter of Alhaji Mainasara Maikudi Dankano', she said rather quietly.
'What', not finding words, 'You the daughter to the sugar magnate! I said with some awe.
'So tell me, where are you going to in Abuja? She beckoned trying to change the topic.
'Garki', I replied.
'Which of the Garki's?
'Area 8! 'But seriously, you don't look like an hausa girl', I said.
She laughed, bringing out from her handbag a cellular phone.
'What else do you have in your magic handbag! I joked.
'Nothing' she replied, while dialing at the same time.

During the few moments left to myself, I thought of giving her something, to keep the relationship aglow, I decided to write her a short poem. Flipping through my dairy, I wrote

      Like a bird lost in the atmosphere
      Not knowing where to turn or going nowhere
      From the deep blue sky
       Came a she-dove bird
        Elegant and splendid
        To pilot the distressed
         To a stress-free abode
        The lost to be found
        Under her elegant wings.

'What's that you are writing? She asked
'Well, am trying to say how, I feel in a poem for you, take it, I have finished.'
'You are quite a poet', she said.
'Thanks', I replied.
'Look at the Abuja Unity Stand, isn't it beautiful? She asked
'It is, Abuja is beautiful but can never be like Lagos', I added
'C'mon don't say that, Abuja is better than Lagos', she argued ' With its serene environment and less chaotic situation, I bet you will live longer in Abuja than in Lagos'. She replied
'Oh yea! I seem to agree.
'When will you come to see me? She asked
'I don't know, its left for you to decide', I put in.
'Decide how? She wanted to know.
'Well, I would be staying in Abuja for five days before going to my posting, so you decide', I said.
The bus had already stopped at it finally bus stop at Jabi and passengers were already disembarking.

'That's our car over there' she said as both highlighted.'
And come over, let me introduce you to my sister, she is also sweet but sometimes saucy.'
Tagging behind 'Laraba met Jeff and Jeff meet Laraba my younger sister.'
'Hi, Jeff'. Laraba greeted
'Hello, hope you don't mind, I call you Lara', I asked
'Yea, I mind cos you make it sound, yoruba'. She replied
'Oh you seem to know the yoruba's' I said
'Well, you can say that and are you Yoruba? She asked
'No', I replied
'Well, till we see again, bye'.
Turning to meet Zainab
'Am sure going to miss you', she said
'Then give me a gift, I won't forget in a hurry'.
She surprised me by planting a kiss on my cheek, right there in public.
'Oh, I thought hausa girls are not suppose to do that? I asked
'We still haven't decided who would visit who first' she said laughing adding 'Why don't you decide'.
I brought out my wallet, in search of my lucky coin but it was no where to be found.
'Zainab dear, I sure can't decide now, I would contact you as to who would visit who first'.
As I saw her leaving, a verse kept crossing my mind
        'The lost to be found
          Under her elegant wings
I hailed a taxi.
'Area 8! I said.
'Two hundred naira', he replied
'Lets go', I said
And I go fulfilled, it sure was a gamble accomplished.

(25)
RAINFALL

The clouds are darken
The winds tune changed
All around a different tempo
Helter-skelter, here and there
Shouts, calling of names
Carrying of valuables.
Running to safety as fast
As ones legs would.

A heavy down pour
It is sending excitement
Down ones spine.
Not too long, little lads
On pants or naked, streamlines
Into the scene; boys of age
Sets stones to play football.---
The heavy downpour backed by
Heavy winds increases the
Excitement. Everywhere screams,
Shouts, so thrilling and enjoyed.
Running up and down
Naked little boys and girls
Holding forth hands
To gather and splash on
Each other.
Fully satisfied and tired
Into ones respective homes
To dry and lay to rest.

(26)
UNBELIEVABLY TRUE

Never had I anticipated
This moment would come

When I would sit alone and feel lonesome.
After all these years together
We are now dispersed
Like the dry leaves
From a fig tree
Blown apart by the east wind.
All the birds have
Left their nest, for the
Great tree which makes
It possible for gathering
Is cut down.
So we would all leave
Each other as it is now.
How unbelievable it was
But in fact a truth.
How painful, the parting,
Tears, sincere heartbreaks.
Many never to be seen
Or heard of again
Forever and ever.
Those times back then
When remembered, a heavy heart.
Those days when remembered
Thrills one with full excitement
Wishing for what would never be.
But life goes on
So lets make the best
Out of whatever is left.
It is so unbelievable but true.

(27)
REMEMBER
Good-for-nothing ingrate

Never-do-well idiot
Foolishly stupid.
On and on it went
Day in day out.
You are thief, a cheat
And a swine.
I alone all this titles?
I felt great anytime
Am being honoured.
Imagine a day not passing
And not been reminded
Of ones supposed specialities
Until I blacked-out.

Horns rimmed the air
Sree, sree, squelching tarring.
Fights for dominance
On the movable lane.
Alone on one side of the road
Stood a woman by her car
My chauffeur packing by her car
'is there a way I can help, madam?'
Turning from the door and look
First dimly, then brightly;
A ricky-rack she was standing by.
It cannot be, was the answer.
'what cannot be madam?'
You, you the …..
She seem to say
The unwanted, irresponsible
On and on it went ones.
'Would you be kind to allow
My chauffeur fix the problem?'
It was like a thunderbolt,

Standing transfixed, not moving.
Not saying a word, annihilatedly
Moved. A ghost come back to life.

I felt high, to see
Her like that, so she remembered?
What has become of her since?
I never want to know,
Only that the wheel of fortune
Spinned the other way round.
Her throwing me out was for good
Not realizing.

I feel good knowing she lost
Everything, but I don't her bad too
Her once beautiful face
Now a feature of old painting.
I would always remember
The encounter
The title giver
The lioness now annihilated.

(28)
JUST REALISING
I am just realizing
This façade of indulgence
A one time desire
I lost out
It ruined me
Blindly foreseeing
Holding steadfastly to that one desire
Paying it out later on.

All those times
I was with you, never was steady
Not calm to think straight
Anxious cavorting, caddish views
Open display of my next move
Not realizing its folly then.
I just realized
Reviewing those your hungry looks
Your derilous convocation
And my unsettled being
Not realizing the yearnings.
The innate groaning for my being
Losing thereafter doubly.

Oh! I wallah
At my folly
My inconsiderable loss
My one opportunity.

You had a lord
But wanted my lordship
Open display, unashamedly.
Even in that lone angle
Holding my hands, moving lower;
You had said
'How manly handsome you are'.
I didn't blush but was blind,
The fire in your eyes
The tightening of your lips
The increasing pressure of your breasts.

Still I did not realize
I could have tasted

Of your apply juice pond
Eaten enough of your
Full grown and ripened grapes.

I feel like hitting
My head on the wall.
Why did I not realize
Your dying desire for my lordship?
Showing that I care then
But really caring now.
Enjoying what I should have had
Only now in my illusion.
Now that you are gone
Far, far away
Not seeming to reach out
Not seeming to feel again.

(29)
RESUMPTION

Back in those days
When resumption was breath-taker
And a scene- maker.
Sight seers, window shoppers.
Leaving ones mouth to water.
All ears of clattering/blattering
Impressive dummies, exotic artiste
All in a classless quirk.
Intriguing yet disdainful
 A scene for valued art.
All beefed up with rosy cheeks,
Well polished, spotless all over.
Dry scales, heavily tanned
But still reflecting considerably.

The elation undefined
With egoistic display of
Accessories. Adventures relayed,
Stories cooked up with added spice
All in the effervence of the
Atmosphere. But is of a temporal
Reunion.

The excitement over
The sixth sense at alert
The struggle of the days follows
Weather beaten, hunger beaten
Material beaten, whole being sunken.
Alertly desperate
A survival of the meanest
The ants being the wisest
 Saved for cold days.

Going back now
The annals of the period
Seems a heavy relief.
The policing, the brutality,
The mischievousness, the disgraces
The ant niggard.
The tribalistic condensation
All the effigy of our being
Demoralized, destroyed
Broken by supposed builders,
Forgery an acquiensce of misinformation.
Then the period to cavort around
With only the covering of the body.
Beaming with smiles, clattering/blattering.
For the interlude.

(30)
MY HOME

My home is
My weakness, my strength
My misfortune, my fortune
My redeemer.
Looking at my home
It is the intersident of fate.
Freedom an epitome of
My home.
Not being obliged
However to anyone, following time
As wished.
Nothing as having yours
As yours.
For ours can be ours
But mine is mine.
Your freedom is always
Limited off home.
If not under verbal scrutiny,
Physical scrutiny.
For my home, there seem no substitute.

(31)
ACHABA SPLENDOUR

Another day
Like all other days.
The struggle continues
For it is a world
Where survival is for the meanest.
Having high hopes of
Making good the latter

To beat the former.
So here it is going into the day.
All sweet over
All scent cover
Easing the tension of the moment
At back, comfortably seated
A beauty with all parts complete
The temptation irresistible
Slyishly conjouring any opportunity
To appreciate the rendavous.
But still eating the miles
Continuous slyish jerks
Full forward, sit tight
All space consumed
Don't blame me, I suffer
My pole to interlude
Transmission. A way to
Easing the hot tension
Of a long day intermission.
I go back filling proud
The figure eight an easy lay
Now in my coffer.

(32)
RISING

The dawn is come
Fair, frail daughter.
A beginner of new beginnings.
I couldn't have forgotten
Those days and times
Spent together;
We were but novice beginners.
The memories, those events
Still vividly in mind.

And I never realized
Not until now
The once little bird
Now eagerly ready to fly.
Ready to test its wings
In the open field.
But remember
Sweet sixteen
Fly cautiously and high
Avoid desperate shoot outs
Which breaks the wings
Leaving one helpless.

The dawn is come
And the stage already set
Oh frail daughter.
Oh sweet sixteen
For today a lady of fairness,
With a heightened tempo for adventure
Feeling its time
But not yet time.
Remain cautious, with open eyes
Or fall prey to lurking lions.
To be broken
To pieces and devoured
Recklessly.
In this new beginning of a beginner.

(33)
LEVELS

I practiced from night to morn
On tactics to woo you.

I hardly had slept
When morn showed its face.
But when I saw you
Later on
I lost all companions with me.

(34)
MYSTERY LADY

Everyday I see you
I wonder who you are
Everyday you walk by
I am thrilled by your vibe.
I tried inquiring
But none seem to know you.
So I got prepared to break
This stunning puzzle.
And since then I never
Saw you again.

(35)
I FEEL LIKE…..

I feel like jumping
On you anytime I behold your presence.
I feel like holding
You, dancing round and round.
I feel like kissing
You, from top to floors.
I feel like caressing
You, all over, wherever, whenever.
I feel like, I feel like
Holding you, jumping on you
Kissing you, caressing you
Holding unto you tightly

Never letting go.

(36)
HOW I FEEL

My words are not enough
To explain how I feel.
My thoughts are not enough
To contain how am feeling.
My actions are never enough
To express my utmost feeling.
But one day, somehow
I would fully express
How you make my whole being feel.

(37)
SUFFER

Gone are the days
Of rising bells and
Shouting mauraders.

Beasts in human form
Caring less not minding
The circumstances.
Paraded in the early frosty
Morning, after being leveled
To full alert.

Having nothing on but
 A loin as clothing
Instead of a heavy blanket
And sweater to put on.

My parents are poor
What can I do?
Nothing! But to continue
Laying on my iron
Blanket bed.
Looking out for the beasts
Mauraders.

(38)
ONE TURN....

One turn as dem say
Good for another.
You do me good,
You go get good.
And if na bad
You go get am for bad too.
So do the thing
Wey you sabi am do.
But make you all time
Put for back of mind.
One turn as dem say
Good for another.

(39)
MEH UNA NO VEX

Meh una no vex
All the time weh I dey block block una.
Meh una no vex
For even di fight fight dem.
Meh una no vex
For all di correct correct
Weh I bin tink say una like.
Look! Mr, wetin be di use
For di fight fight

For di correct correct?
Wey all dem wey
You dey fight fight
You dey correct correct
For, no want and like am.

(40)
LET HER KNOW

Tell her
    Let her know, if you see her.
Those times I was alone
Wishing solemnly for her.

Tell her,
    Let her know, when you see her.
Those times I want to hold
But a mirage.

Tell her,
    Let her know, when you see her
Those words I so would
 Love to tell her.

Tell her,
    Let her know, when you see her.
Those conversatory notes
I daily fantasied of us both.

For in knowing
Would you understand
How I always felt
When not with you.

(41)
LOOKING AT HER

Looking at her
She is so full of beams.
Radiatingly glowing
A rare gem.
Looking at her.

(42)
STATIC

Sitting on the edge
Of life.
I reviewed my life.
What is the cause?
Who is to blame?
I am the cause
I am to blame
For the flame
Which burns
Deep in my within.
For am neither up
Nor am I down.
Am equilibry unbalanced.
For one thing holds me
From my ups.
Sitting on the edge
Of life
As I review my life.

(43)
ARISE! BE UNIFIED

They are all blacks
Under the same polity

Pursuing different causes
Through malign pronouncement
Crucial enough to disable the whole polity
In a bid to express their God cursed
Liberties.
Beating drums of war
For ignorant minded fools
To dance out in misguided compassion
Showcasing their lust in misrepresented passion.

How long brothers?
Would we continue
To be used by sucking vampires.
How long
Should we continue
Living a mirage unity
In a land where everyone is for himself
In a land where honesty is not the best policy.
It has become a national anthem
If you cannot beat them
Better join them.
For honesty is jeered at
Dishonesty praised to the high heavens.
You have to soil your hands to be worthy.

Tell me this one thing!
Why should I sit down and watch
Corruption recycling corruption?
At the detriment of honesty
At the detriment of our collective unity.
Arise from your slumber,
And come together.
From the east, west, north, south.
Let us rebuild Nigeria.

Patriotic physicians come with your tools
And lets heal this decadence
Eating deep into the polity's soul.
Why sit and watch!
These pompous I don't careism
These disguised war call.
Religion suffering the brunt of man's greed.
Arise! It is no time for siddon look.

(44)
TO BE A MAN

Boy-Man- I'm now a man
          Grown in height
          Filled in necessary parts
          My grasses are getting
          Thicker and thicker
          Day by day
          More under my check bone.
Old-Man- Boy you are but
          At the very first step
          Of a normal process.
Boy-Man- Never, I can tune
          My radio, getting the
          Right station.
          Washing thrice daily
          Blessing myself with
          Sweet smelling scents.
Old- Man- It is all but
          The first step
          Of greater things
          Coming.
Boy-Man – No, not at all
          I shack, one, two
          I burn smoke's

Old-Man – To be my level
What's more!
Never be deceived
Boy. Manhood is all about ups
and down.
Boy-Man – Tell me then
Wise one, the path
To be followed?
Old- Man – One cannot be bigger
Than ones self. Wisdom,
Understanding, is a potential
Tool to being matured.
Being knowledgeable
Inspires confidence
And not those things around you.
Being matured has its sacrifice.

(45)
THE QUEST SEEKERS
(20 February/20 October)

It was as a festival of bonfire
A random mid-summer fiesta
A pique rag day siniter
Of restive motion for sight seer's.
 But the dogs were watching
 Salivating and waiting.
The Mc climbed a stage
Announcing a change in venue
Accompanied with a change of tune
And the heaven blessed the day
But the tensed fun remains unchanged.
 Now the dogs were rumoured loose
 To bite and bark fuse.
During the interlude transit

Awaiting the Dj's next hit.
The proprietor say's he's done with,
Thereby creating a tight sit
And a panorama for knuckle-fist
    For the dogs were expected
    And a dicey welcome inadverted
The hysterism was nightmarish
As barkings filled the air
A madness condusive in a psychiatric
Environment.
Getting intoxicated with weep wine,
This drunkenness, sets many on their heels
To be sober, pms came in handy.
    The dogs were on prowl
    Barking and biting flow
On that 8th in 9th in 20 millennium one/20 in 10 in 20 millennium 20
Former in defiance of school authority interference
Latter endsars public protest.
When the sun was set,
The sheeps were scattered
Only few headed the call of the
Shepherds.
Cause the spirit has left already.
    For the baying mastiffs
    Has ravaged and spoiled
    With all gladness
    With all tidemen
The captain and his crew
Click clacking with boisterious
Haw haw of self condemnation.
On course a chart to self destruction.
But by togetherness, when the time is due
Shall we overcome and a new dawn renew.

Let the dogs wail
We shall wait
Let the dogs bark
We shall bait
For its rightful place
Is in the cage.

(46)
DESPERATE MUGU

She swings her hips
Like the palm tree dancing to
The rhythm of the wind.
A ca' la' ma' gbo'! An exhilaration
When she turns her front side
Seeing her full grown ripen grapes
Resting on a well carved edifice.
Your shrinking pole charges
To full alert.
Savouring her in your thoughts
With no strength to go say hi.
This paragon of beauty
You won't kill me before my time.
For I must get to you
Even it cost me my last dime.

(47)
DOMITTILA

I know you somewhere
Me, no not me
But you were the one
I met at uniben?
Now you missed your way,
Anyway, I once went there.

Please do you mind
Giving m your address?
Sure, why not, take, here it is.
On a good day
 I went searching, searching
For the goddess, I saw on my way.
House 102, 42nd avenue, red light district.
I got there
What!
There she was, skimpily dressed
A lighted stick at hand
In broad day light
Standing by a pole
Her other hand on her hips
Negotiating.

(48)
AFRO WESTERNER

They are comfortable, confidently satisfied,
Babbling away in foreign tongues.
They feel irritated
When greeted in their native tongue;
Always twisting their tongue
As if hot coal rests on top
When wanting to speak.
They are uncomfortable with their colour
Bathing also in corrosive waters
Washing away beauty black
Becoming neither black nor white.
Justifying their ignorance in so called civilization.
What is civilization without tradition?
Reforming your roots is civilization.

ii

Son of my father

Daughter of my mother,
Long ago, our ancestors
Our ancestors were crated away
Away across the ocean.
Generations after generations
Having lost their heritage
Coined for themselves a new appendage.
Foreign to our culture,
Strange to our tradition.
All in a bid to rediscover
A long lost heritage.

iii

In our virgin land
There has arisen a breed
Right in the midst of Africa
So full of traditions undiluted
So full of culture unrefined.
Fools who jeer at the Africaness of Africa.
Preferring the ways of outsiders.
Dispelling what our brothers
Across the ocean longs for with all sincerity.
Becoming intoxicated with western pollution
Shoving aside the richness of our Africaness.
Becoming westernly minded
Becoming westernly sounded.
This Afro-westerners.

iv

You have the white man's ways
You have the white man tongue
But you have your brain

And your blood still runs black.
Do not annihilate totally
But tend to appreciate solely
Our ancestral heritage
Which has been plundered
And crated away, long, across the sea.
Making themselves inferior
In order not to rediscover themselves
So as to recover.

V

Live me to appreciate my heritage
Which you jeer at
There lies your rot
In the land of your root
And see what, I would make
And see what, I would make
Of my heritage.

(49)
LET THOSE WITH EARS HEAR

I thought,
    With the ousting of draconian rule
     We will head ahead to the promiseland
      But how far would we get
    With this present head?
My thinking! How far?
I thought,
    You made mention of not being our messiah
    Yet still sit on the pilot sit
     With grandiose display of vainglorious
piousness
    To the piety.

        Hearing that sonorous gruff
        Makes me grief.
This thinking! How far.
I thought,
        You are treading jejely-jejely
        And moving slowly slowly
        Which is in favour of a section
        Of the polity.
        Are others insignificant?
My thinking! How far.
I thought,
        You pride yourself
        As the bringer of change
        And feel mad about ipob
        But folder your arms
        When terrorist herdsmen
        Were killing, kidnapping, raping and maiming
Innocent citizens
        And only saying 'accommodate your brothers'
        Are we but in the same polity?
This thinking! How far.

I thought,
        With your rigging back for second term
        Things would be better.
        I know it would not just happen
        This is why we need to restructure
        And build for a better tomorrow.
This thinking! How far.
I thought,
        Young boys would start thinking
        Maturedly and shun all nocturnal act
        Which only leads to the gallow
        And young girls behaving responsibly

  Lessening their population on Allen
  Aminu Kano and……
  Parents showing more
  Concern for the well-being of their off-springs
  Or get ready for asocial explosion.
My thinking! How far.
I thought,
  All those in the rural areas
  Would now be educated
  And all those ignoramus
  On why their votes should not be sold.
  Having respect for the law.
  Even though, the head of the polity
  Is a despoiler of the law,
  Who wants the rule of law
  To come secondary to national security.
This thinking! How far.
My thoughts,
  Are simple and straight forward
  To truly have a home.
  Travelling from North to South
  East to West without fear or discrimination.
  When even in ignorance
  There would be empowerment.
  And the upholder of law
  Would respect service to humanity
  And the populace respecting
  And upholding the law.
  And let those in authority
  Become more sensitive
  To the masses plight.
This my thinking! How far.

(50)
SUCH REMEMBRANCE

Sweet heart, always remember
  The day we met
  The things we said
  Dreams yet to come to pass.
  Forever, you would be mine
  Holding you in that deepest
  Part of my holy of holies.
  I would always love you
  As long as I breathe.

(51)
SO ALONE

I am so alone
Tossing from one end to the other.
I feel so alone
Waking up and knowing you are gone.

(52)
MY LOVE

Beau,
    Where are you?
    Where can I find you?
    I want you by my side
    To make me feel
    That special way
    Which is uniquely your touch.
    Come and arouse me
    Taking me to heights
    Yet unreached
    Discovering planets
    Yet undiscovered.

(53)
TORTURE CHAMBER

My jasmine,
I have gone to hell
For you.
I have conquered demons
For your sake.
I have triumphed
All for you.
Now is the time
Yet you hold back
From me, the best of you.

(54)
MY HEART WOULD GO ON

My heart would go on
Far distances, miles after miles.
Knowing you are there for me.
My heart would sail on
Across wide seas and
Across large oceans
To berth at your bossom.

(55)
CROSS ROAD

Where are we going?
Tell me, where are we going?
I look around
And feel very lost.
At this junction
It seems to be
That the fortunate
Are getting more fortunate

The unfortunate becoming
More unfortunate.
For the sun meant for all
Shines only on a few.
And the little ray pouring on us
Is gradually losing its lights.

Oh my mother!
Where do I go?
What should I do?
Oh my father!

When the rays of the sun
Is stolen for leaving doomer days
It is not yet felt cause
Of the seeming abundance of sunrays.

Alas, doomer days lurks
Around the corner.
Awake! Lest you get
Caught unaware.

(56)
KNOWING WHO

You don't know me
Do not say you know me?
I am the opposite, your idea of me.
I am slippery, sleekish and sly as a snake.
Wise yet sometimes foolish.
Calm yet aggressive.
Meek yet stubborn.
An angel yet a demon.
Interchanging as sunrise and sunset.

But still you say you know me?
Tell me what I would do next?
Tell me what I will not do next?
I am what you should not think
I am but neutral.

(57)
IF ONLY

If only I can have you
You would be the center of my world.
You would be the light that shine
In my darkness.
You would be my inspirati
And my only true desire.
I won't let you down cos
I would always listen to your heart.
You would have nothing to far.
It would be you and only you always.
If only I can have you.

SHORT STORY (3)
WHAT GOES AROUND, COMES AROUND

Tyson sat on a couch in the sitting room watching a musical video clip but really his mind was somewhere else, he was brooding over taye's success at hitting it big and now the main man in the area.
Thinking aloud, 'What! I don't know what am doing sitting and doing nothing, look at taye, he is now the talk among the guys in the area, men see how he is spending money', 'Well I wouldn't blame him, he's quite lucky coz his father travels a lot especially to Europe and America, so why wouldn't he have the opportunities anyway?'
The doorbell intruded into his thoughts.

'Yes, who is it?' Tyson enquired.
'Its me olboy!'
'Samo Samo, hold on please, I am coming. Going to open the door for his friend Samuel
'Tyson, my man, what's up mhen?' asked Samuel.
They both shook hands multiple times.
'Nothing much, come in'.
'Wait a moment, is your uncle at home?' Samuel asked.
'No, am home alone'. Answered Tyson
'You know, after Timi and I last encounter with that Uncle of yours, men, but tell me, why was he so harsh like that?'
'I don't know what to say, you know this house belongs to him and the way he met us the other day, men, anybody would have been angry'.
'Oh , oh, so playing music, dancing to the music and feeling high is bad now for youths like us? Asked Samuel.
'Look who is a youth, you are not even eighteen yet and already regarding yourself as one'. 'Anyway, leave that matter'.
'Well, we all would soon be eighteen in a couple of months, anyway, like you said, lets forget about that, gosh is that this year musical?'
'It is'.
'Whoa, Nigerian artiste are really trying you know, and it is now being appreciated by the audience'.
'Sure, we are beginning to embrace our own and less of especially American artiste, but wait o, that a new shirt you have on', going closer 'what label is it, come let me see'. Taking a hold of the shirt collar. 'Jesus, that's a Tommy' he exclaimed
'Sure, it's a tommy, Taye bought it for me'. Explained Samuel
'You mean both the shirt and wristwatch designed by

almighty Tommy', Tyson asked surprised.
'Sure, or are you surprised?' asked Samuel
'No not at all'.
'Taye took myself, jeremiah, shola, monica, Julia and ijeoma out last week Saturday to mamet, it was on our way home, he took myself and monica, to the shopping complex, to spoil us some more; you know, I hooked him up with monica and he's quite over his head with her, for now, seeing how with his new found fortune, Taye doesn't last long with any girl'.
'Men, I missed greatly then'.
'It wasn't a small thing oh, Taye was spending as if he owns all the money in central bank'. Enthused Samuel.
Well one wouldn't blame Taye for spending so much, his father makes every fortnight trip to Europe, America, UK and the carribeans, its rumoured that as a financial advisor, actually, he is helping the military guys launder money abroad and so has lot of foreign currencies littered around his house.

Tyson and Taye used to be in the same class from JSS one to three, after their junior waec examination, Taye proceeded to the science class while Tyson went on into the Arts class.
Taye use to be everybody's boy, he was what in local parlance is called a 'mugu', he was always wanting to roll with the happening guys of which Tyson was one of the happening guys.
However, how Tyson and his other happening guys are able to maintain that status was because of some petty deals sometimes bothering on petty household theft they usually conclude and come squander the money in school.
Knowing Taye's father dealings, which was an open

secret, Tyson decided to with the help of Samuel and Jeremiah coopt Taye into pilfering some of his father's hard currency. He was not easily convinced and complained of being afraid and not having the mind to steal.
'Look here Taye, you want to roll with the big boys right?, there is nothing to lose instead there is everything to gain'. Tyson said.
'Moreover, you are the first son, even though you have elder sisters, they don't pose a threat! Jeremiah added.
'Taye, let me tell you one thing you don't know, even if your father knows, he would be confused men, be a fast guy for once, hit as much as you can'. Samuel puts in
'Boy, I don't like talking for too long, are you going to do it or not? Inquired Tyson, already getting angry.
'I would try my best'. Taye finally said.
'Lets go boys and see what would happen! Tyson said.
The boys still felt unconvinced by the reluctant commitment of Taye later in the month ,an opportunity came knocking when Jeremiah's mother arrived from Germany. As a fast guy, he hit a hundred duesch mark.
'Guys, I have some good news'. Jeremiah beckoned on his friends the next day.
'As how? Samuel asked
'My mum is back'. Jeremiah replied.
'Is that so, it's truly good news'. Tyson chipped in.
'Hey guys, take a look at this'. Flipping a note out of his pocket.
'Oh man, you are a fast one, give me five, no ten.' Samuel excited was requesting.
They all shook hands and hugged each other.
'When do we go change it? Jeremiah asked.
'Hold on guys, I have an idea! Tyson puts in
'What is it'. Both inquired

'Taye'. Tyson answered.
Yes Taye. Both answered with understanding.
Eventually, they went to change the Duetshe mark.
'How much do you change one duetche mark'. Inquired Jeremiah from the mallam.
'Fifty naira'. Answered the mallam.
'Common, you want to cheat us, its sixty naira'. Samson replied.
'Haba, you na customer, I no cheat you, it's the price, wallahi'. The mallam answered.
'Lets change it like that, because if we don't he can set us up, you know'. Tyson whispered into Jeremiah's ears.
'Okay, but it is a hundred we want to change'.
'No problem'. The mallam answered 'follow me'.
On getting to his shade.
'Wait outside, you come inside'. Indicating to Jeremiah.
'Men five thousand naira, it isn't much but it is something'. Tyson said.
'So this is how it is done, my father always leaves his foreign currencies carelessly'. Taye puts in.
'Then what are you waiting for.' Tyson said, 'do it and do it fast'.
After blowing the money with Taye, he became pessimistic about the whole affair, Tyson feeling really bad about the supposed delay and felt cheated since it was his idea to bring Taye in so as to build trust and confidence as well as needed motivation, gave Taye the beating of his life, but for the intervention from Jeremiah and Samuel, it would have been another story which would have been told. It was same week Taye hit his millions.
'Look here Samo, I couldn't have wasted my saliva without getting something in return'. Said Tyson
'I quite agree with you, lets forget about small small

things, ;look Taye is hosting a pool bash this Saturday at sagura hotels, come and have fun and make up with the guy, there is money now, lets spend it with him before the bubble burst'. Samuel enthused.
'Sure, why not!
'But, how about your uncle?
'Uncle ko, Uncle ni, I will find a way around it, or has excuses ended in this world'.
They both laughed.
'Men, I better be going'. Samuel said. Standing up from the chair.
'You want to go, why don't you stay a little longer?
'Ah, I see you hate me, so your uncle when he comes and sees me here, to... my neck, thank you'. Replied Samuel.
'Anyway when are you visiting again? Asked Tyson
'Why ask me, when are you coming to my own place? Replied Samuel.
'Ok, I will be there tomorrow'.
'Tomorrow, you said, I would be expecting you'.
'Till tomorrow then'.
'Till morrow bye.
Closing the gate.

At the party that weekend with the whole place boisterous and filled with gaiety and the DJ churning out the latest musical hits.
'Guys, do you know my uncle has traveled! Asked Tyson
'No, not at all! Both answered.
'He traveled to the UK last night and won't be back until three weeks from today, wasn't even in the picture of his travel plans'.
'Hey, guys, you are missing the main part of the party'. A voice cuts in.
'T, for Tayeeeee! Hailed Jeremiah

'Hi, Tyson', Taye extending his hands towards Tyson.
'Maintain, am out this afternoon to enjoy myself, nothing more'. Stating Tyson
'See, I have forgotten everything that happened'.
'Ah, I see you have really matured'. Mocked Tyson.
'Hey, guys, lets forget all this and let bygone be bygone! Intervened Samuel.
'That's what am trying to do! Answered Taye.
'Hey, Jerry boy am at the counter'. Tyson said leaving.
'Whats wrong with him?', 'if he doesn't want peace, then why is he at my party? Inquired Taye angrily.
'Forget it, Taye, Tyson is not in the mood right now but I assure you, he would come around'. Puts in Samuel.
'Okay then lets enjoy the party.' Taye concluded.
The party was really big, everything was available and the DJ was just slamming the jukebox properly, churning out the right songs. Everywhere was hot and tight with enough teen girls in bikinis, splashing around in the pool and just milling around coupled with enough chewables. It was the bomb.
'Tyson, why don't you just forget all about what transpired between you both and enjoy the pay while it last.' Jeremiah shared
'Gosh you still don't understand me then, that was a serious act meant to be nothing by doing so, when we eventually reconcile fully, the respect would naturally be there.' Answered Tyson. ' I don't hold anything especially after today, seeing all this'.
'Chai, you are funny! Chipped in Jeremiah.
'lets enjoy while it lasts'. Tyson enthused.
Tyson's uncle eventually came back three weeks later with a total sum of fifty thousand pounds sterling, on finding out about this, Tyson took all the money.
'Guys, my uncle is back. Informed Tyson

'Oh yea, then goodies has landed'. Cuts in Samuel.
'Sure take a look inside the bag'.
'Whao, this is hot men, how much is that altogether/ asked Jeremiah.
'Fifty thousand'. Replied Tyson.
'Gosh, that's close to a million buck you know'. Samson replied.
'Sure, its close to a million.' Replied Tyson.
'O man, whats to be done now? Asked Jeremiah
'We all will go to Port-harcourt and paint the city red.' Tyson answered.
'Wait, what about your remaining exams, you know we are done with our waec? Asked Samuel
'Forget about that, ive already taken care of it, you guys know Kingsley'. Asked Tyson
'Sure'. Both answered
'He is sitting the remaining papers for me'. Tyson informed
'Gosh, you sure are fast. Replied Samuel.
Shaking hands and hugging each other.
'To Port Harcourt then'. Enthused Tyson.
'To the garden city' they both chorused.
Ha ha ha ha ha, they all laughed.

The sun rose and shone like any other day bright and warm with two lovers enjoying the early rays as it serenade into their bodies.
'Look here Janet, I would take you to the end of the world, just be rest assurred'. Tyson was saying.
A knock on the door broke the conversation.
'Who is that'. Tyson asked
'Its us'
'Baby, please go open the door for my guys'.
Samson and Jeremiah walks into the room looking down.

'Whats up guys, I thought you were out with the girls relaxing......... walking from behind into the room was Tyson's uncle and some five mean looking men.
'What uncle, wha- what are you doing here'. Jumping from the bed.
'What's happening here? Inquired Janet.
'It's no problem! Replied Tyson's uncle, 'I never knew you could be so mean, after everything I have done for you, well where is the remaining money? He asked.
'It's finished'.
'You want to play with me or do you think am joking, travelling all the way from Abuja to come here stories, if you know what's good for you, release the remaining money left'. Explained his Uncle.
'Uncle, I mean it, everything is finished'.
His friends just stood there thinking how on earth Tyson's uncle located their whereabout.
'T.T, Iron, guys deal with this rat for me'. His uncle commandeered.
'Okay, please hold on, it is in the wardrobe'. Standing up to go get it.
'How much is left/'. Asked his uncle
'A hundred and twenty or less'. Retrieving same and handing it over.
'You know what, I wouldn't do anything to you, just pack your bags and baggages and you two do likewise.' Ordered Tyson's uncle
In the detention facility in which Tyson was locked up in.
'Chai, I left fifty thousand naira under the mattress how would I get out of this place and go retrieve the money now', thought Tyson ' and nothing pains me more than the loss of the money, not even this rotten place; I just hope Jeremiah and Samuel's parents have heard what happened.

At the police station, both parents were present to bail their sons.
Crying profusely, 'I ve always told Jeremiah not to be following bad boys, now see what he has put himself into'. Jeremiah's mum was saying and crying.
'Shut up woman, where you not the one that spoilt him'. Replied his Father angrily, 'let him come out first, I would....'
At that same time the Divisional Police Officer (DPO) strolled into his office, all stood up at once, heading toward his office.

(58)
FLASHBACK

Sure I remember those times
When you made me fill inferior
Always looking down on me
Calling a small rat.

I sure do remember
Those back slaps
Those calling of boy run up
I wasn't wise then.

How long it has been?
I do not know
But can vividly remember
All the dog master game.

For time really flies
Creeping slowly like a snail
Then catching up quite unaware
Making one unprepared.

You were surprised seeing me
Why be surprised, you thought
You were better than me
No! how time flies.

(59)
TAIL GATE FOR DEAR LIFE

I am at the edge
Of really break down
Fear of the unknown
Horrific thoughts
At tail gate for dear life.

Reluctant to leave
Not knowing how it
Means or feels to leave.
Indocxicated in ferocious syllables.
Why am I so uncertain,
So afraid, a feel of guilt
At tail gate for dear life.

But I bounce back
Fully rejuvenated
Caring les for the unknown
Fully prepared and ready to conquer
At tail gate for dear life.

(60)
GOD SAVE THE DEAD (Honour of the Nyanya Bomb Blast)

Heavy traffic
Network jamming

Loved ones inquiring
Siren blaring
Dead ferried
Same spot twice thunder struck
Panick mode activated
Worry women's bread and butter.
Confident men maintain balance
Divine mercy all pray.
God save the dead.

(61)
BELOVED

What are you doing now
I cannot tell
Trying to bring in the reveries
Of yesterday to fit today.
Oh brothers!
My heart is heavy
Not wanting to think harshly
For ours is ours; but yours is yours
Of the going on over there.
All arrows shot got me
But only a few really hurt me
Wounding me almost beyond repair.
But I overcame it all.
Learn from me, learn from it,
I have taken all wounds
Meant for us.
Thrive continuously, you would make it.

My heart is heavy
Liking you as antelops
In the midst of lions
But be as the serpent
Open-eyed, wise and sharp
Never taken for granted.
It is bravery not to be caught
Than to be caught.

(62)
THIS SOMETHING

There is something about you
I cannot grasp, but feel to grasp.
Those silent looks of yours,
A surrounding aura of sel-confidence.
Putting me far, yet am so near.
This nearness, I feel to grasp
This grasp, I feel deep in down me.
Having this want of being overwhelmed,
By those eluding eyes.
Wanting to feel those velvety warmth
Of those tender palms, his creator
Bestowed on you.
That self-comportment
Of this composed elegance
A paragon of beauty.
Arising in me, this elm of imagination

Igniting in me this feel to grasp
This something about you.

(63)
REAPER

The rain that drops from the skies
Return back to the skies.
The farmer who left
His home for the farm
Would return back
Home from his farm.
But words spoken
Cannot return
But moves to establish
Itself, on the soft-soil
 Of the mind
 To grow and
 Strengthen its hold
Unless forgiven.

(64)
LUST

How am feeling
I don't know
Only this I know
You stir up something
Deep down my inside

Stirring me to craziness.
Exciting my lust
Making me hot
Making me lost
For caring for you,
Making me crazy
For this lust, I feel.
Reach out to me….
Save this sinking soul.

(65)
BLOOMING FLOWER

Roses, this roses,
Who would
Grow to blossom
To be scented
To be plucked
To be sucked.

(66)
NOTHING DREAMS

All there is yet
Are nothing but dreams
Sweeping away like the frail clouds
In this squalor
I know
And exist in.

(67)
FEBRUARY 28

It all began
It just began
Within a twinkle of one's eyes
The burning, the maiming
The killing, mass slaughtering.
The confusion, connotation, confrontation.
Aghast, dumbfounded, terrified, speechless.
As the horid events unfold.
Pronouncing fear in every word
Suspicious of every move
Shouts hysteric,
The very bane of the soul dymystified
From dawn until dusk, until dawn, until dusk, until dawn, until dusk.
Doing of frenzied dances
Snorting barbaric display of fanatic religionism
Sharia soldiers, Christian crusaders.
Until the interlude.

(68)
DRUNKEN SOUL

I sat
   Glacing into space
Reviewing my life
   As I gaze

Into the drunkenness of my
   Thoughts
  Reveries of past undoings
Rolling pass my vision
 As I sit
Finding myself
Relieving the past
   That past
I thought
I thought
I had left behind
  Finding out
I'm not myself...
Seem like someone else
So I ask
Myself
What way forward?
This way
I must follow
To free myself
To save my soul.
This drunken soul,
It is from undoing of past.
I am not
Finding my feet
In an effort
To be along

Along that path
Heading for destruction
So I sat
I reviewed my life!
Where do I stand?
Having no platform
To stand...
On mundane ground
Knowing a passing mirage.
I write
Out of confusion
As I try desperately
To save my soul
From this drunkenness
I see!
I know!

(69)
SATISFACTION

Surrounded by an empty fullness
Undescribable yet descriptive
Unimaginable yet imagined
A contentment, so overwhelming
Like love bursting out a champagne bottle
Like kitten playing on the plain grassland.
Felt only in the abysmal depth

Of ones being.
A delirious sensation of contentment
Never known, never felt, never encountered.
Seeing a beauty
Of life
A life worth really living.
For I step out
Of darkness depth.
Standing on the platform
Of heightened light
Radiatingly glowing
In the sensation
Of here.
Finding a reason
To live life on.

(70)
BLACK QUEEN MOTHER

Oh Mother
Black earth upon
Which my feet
I stand firm.
You who is, am dressed.
You who is, am feed.
Like atlas upon whose
Shoulder the world rest.
Unlike mother hen
Desertation is not

Your portion.
You who was, I was.
You who is, I am.
Mother.
I would continue
To envisage you
Now, till kingdom come
I would continue
To cherish you
Now unto eternity.
Let me continue
To hold
To that pillar post.
My strength.
You who is, am educated.
You who is, am liberated.
Mother
Your strength shall
Not wean.
Evolution shall evolve
Its full cycle
Then glory shall
Fully bloom.
Then your seat
Shall be covered
With lilies and roses
And your strength

Come to berth.
Then with head high
Would you sing
Halleluyah.

(71)
MY FLOWER

My flower
Is a delicate
Early spring blossom
Fragile and fair
Endlessly ethereal.
Deeper azure of higher ups
With lips of soft shell pink
With eyes of the night sky
Absorbing not the light
As darker eyes do
But throwing it back
Everytime you turn
Your head
Making reflections
Like still-water
Touched by moonsilver.

My flower
You cure the black
Sickness in my heart

Like a cry in the bitter
Darkness of my heart
With sweetness of face.
If it be a crime
To love you
I gladingly
Plead guilty
If only I be sentenced
To the gallow of your heart.

(72)
HIS MOST HIGH

His most high
Has had me
Redeemed
Liberated
Assured
And fulfilled.
I need no more shake
I need no more panic
I need no more fear
Cos his most high
Has given the word.
Though I a poor sinner
He has given his word.
And given me a new name
ONOSEMUDIANE (One who God stands with).

(73)
HIS REFLECTION

His infinity is overwhelming
His kindness ever flowing
He radiates his peace
With his word
'peace be upon you'
And judges accordingly.

We seem him far
But he is so near
You reach out; touch
'worship with all your heart'
'love your neighbor as yourself'
For we are his reflection
In evolution.

(74)
LOVE

Love is not rushed
But is gentle and calm
Like the cool evening breeze
From the sandy sea shore.

Love is not harsh
But is mild and tender
Like petroleum jelly
On the palm of my mother.

Love is not blind
But is inspiring and motivating
Like a goal just scored
By your favorite football team.

Love is not cold
But is warm and soothing
Like getting your massage
From your inbuilt spa.

Love is not ashamed
But bold and loud
Like the calabar carnival
So colourful, fun and fare.

Love is not bitter
But sweet and refreshing
Like the taste of honey
Of which your lips are coated with.

(75)
NO TIME IS LATE

No time is late
A minute to midnight
Even if it strikes
To your door step

You would still get
And be in safety.

No time is late
Though darkness cover the sky
It would pass on
To open a clear blue sky.

No time is late
Though you feel left behind
But the race is not over yet
Or have you stopped breathing?

No time is late
Though you toil from dusk till dawn
And feel all is nought
Hold tight on and get there.

No time is late
The world is a cycle
Your worst today
Tomorrow will be your best.

No time is late
For after the tears
Comes the cheers
And a testimony on the lips of many.

No time is late
As long as you are steadfast
Your sweat shall sprout sweet fruits
And your head raised up high.
No time is late
Put yourself in your tomorrow
After the wind has blown
And this water has flown.

(76)
THINKING OF YOU

Just sitting
  Thinking of you
    Fills me with
      Euphoric tinglings
        A wanting for closeness
         A wanting for warmness
Just sitting
  Thinking of you.

                II

It is so lovely
Sitting and thinking
Of you.
It is so marvelous
Stretching of hands
And knowing

You are there.

III

How would I feel
With not a thought
Of you every passing day?
You are sweetness made
Manifest.

(77)
VISION

Once,
    Like a shadow
        From a darkmorn
Look close
        Recognize
Well one
          Others
              Amongst.
Closer
    Again
        Familiarise
Smile
    Wean
        Appearance
            Appreciate.

Closest
     Now
A longing
A wanting
For lasting
Ever.
Why?
    Dan Allah
Be mine
      Now
         Again
            Ever
               More.
Ever
   Celebration
        Of
          Celestic
            Balming.
            A
            Joining
            Of
            One
            And
            One
            Now
            One.

(78)
WELCOME BACK

Welcome back
From long ago idleness
Of long ago sullenness.

Welcome back,
From waiting and wailing
Of counseling and consulting
Eyes glued to clock 9 news
For ready news, for prepared ears.

Welcome back,
From the scrabbling for the days
Headlines.
Of long imposed insomnia
Of suspense prolonged comfortably.

Welcome back,
To flank loquacious ostentations
To delirious exhilarated complacent
To this naïve acquiesce.

Welcome back,
To the hustling and bustling
In lecture thearters.
To the scavenging of scavengers

Materials.
Of adroit synchronization in
Confusion of direction.

Welcome back
From excitement overdue
To excitement renewed
Getting down to business
With all seriousness
Getting down to business
With all laxity.

After the long waiting
And long praying
Of demeaned enthusiasm
Of running from Lts
To mock- court.
From LTs to Faculty.
From LTs to Lts.
But still moving along in this
Predestined motion.

I welcome you.

(79)
SOOTHING BALM

Describing you

This elegance
Dymystified.
Your look
Is assurance.
Your build
Is confidence.

Your appearance
Is ethereal.

Your eyes
Is adoration.

Your lips
Subtlety.

You
My fountain
Of peace.

Let me
Forever behold
Your presence
Diana's daughter.
And let
My heart
Rest at bay

Just knowing
You are mine.

(80)
NAUGHTY

Should I look
At you more
Closely
Angel of mine?
With those eyes
Beholding your
Meteoric beauty
Overshadowed by your
Heavenly glamour
Like the rays of
The full moon.

Let my being
Be enshrouded
In your
Euphoric presence.

Let me sail
Lady of mine
To berth
At your bay

To rest at your
Harbor.

(81)
IN HIS PRESENCE

Silence,
Hush; silence
Be silent.
Listen,
Pay attention
Be alert.

For his presence
Is here.
Feel it
Touch it
Envelop in it
Then alone would
You be overwhelmed
By his encompassing
Peace!
This peace
Which takes
Away all
Infirmities
Making me

Whole.
Making me
Complete.
Establishing your
Strides.
Magneting
Favor
Left
Right
Centre.Flowing in confidence
Intuitively perceptively
Connected.Knowing that
In his presence,
His very presence
You only have
To be silent
To feel
To touch
To be made whole
To be established.

(82)
JUST AWESOME

He sits
Next step
Watching

Waiting.

He is a patient being
Supernatural as he is
Not unnecessarily
Interfering
But watching
And waiting.

Until you
Knock
Until you
Open.
Know, his love
Is superfluous.

SHORT STORY (4)
CUNNY MAN DIE, CUNNY MAN BURY AM

I have known No steady for sometime now, he is nothing but a bag full of rubbish. Anywhere he happens to be, everyone just knows he was around. His boastful nature and incapacity to sometimes prove his claims, made guys to nickname him 'No steady'.

Musa but popularly called No steady is a guy who can make you angry and at the same time make you happy. He was always trying to do what naturally he was incapable of doing, a wanting to feel among attitude.

Seeing him or hearing him talk, one cannot but laugh as No steady was always full of words. Like one day he was gisting us of his many designers wears.

"men, the time I bought my levi's top, it was five thousand naira and I have two, even when tommy hasn't started to reign, it was sold for fifteen thousand naira a top, I phoned my aunt in America and she sent me two of it', Musa called No steady was saying.

'Haba, stop bottling us, No steady, you na proper Nigerian bottling company, someone who doesn't know you would enter your bottle and you would just cover it and throw it away', a boy puts in.

'Which one is yours in this matter now? Asked No steady, 'carry your akpola go rest for one place' continued No steady.

'Look at the person that has three nautica, two tommy tops and four levi's jeans and two wrangler jeans, see what he is putting on, your shoe sef, its one in town', the boy replied and bending down to touch No steady's shoes. Everyone bursted into laughter.

'What is the name of the trainers you are putting on, is it pila, fila, pela or fela', asked the boy further

'Aba made'! Someone else answered from the group.

Everyone bursted into laughter. I think No steady met his match on that day but he was not bothered, still carrying on with his gist.

On another day, we were sitting at the front veranda of a friend's barbing salon, admiring the flashy cars driving pass along the highway.

'Men check out that vitara jeep, isn't it cool? I asked

'its cool, that's the kind of jeeps meant for young guys'. Tony puts in.

'All jeeps are good for young guys', ikenna replied

'I know, I only was referring to the lightness and the compatibility of this very jeep' Tony defended.

Heh, look at that lexus jeep? Moses shouted

'why shouting like that, I have seen a jeep with five doors', No steady chips in.

'Eh, you have come again', Ikenna said

As everyone jumped to their feet and burting into laughter, with shouts of No steady, No steady, you don come again. Still Musa No steady remained undaunted and unpertubed.

'If you like believe it or not, I have seen it', replied No steady

'Okay, where did you see it, if I may ask? Someone asked

'When we went to Sheraton hotel in Lagos for lunch' he answered.

'There he goes again, this guy, you are never finished with lies', I replied him

'Allow him, am enjoying him', Jide added.

'If you like believe me, if you like don't believe me, it's you people's problem', he added.

'No steady, No steady', rented the air.
That's Musa for you, he might be telling the truth but his over exaggeration makes it impossible for one to believe what he says.
There again was another day when he said his father had six swiss rolex, each worth about half a million naira each.
'Shout up there', somebody shouted,' hear the way it is sweet coming out of your mouth', mimicking him 'my father has six swiss rolex, each worth about half a million, then what is your father still doing here at garki village?'
'He doesn't even own the house they reside in', volunteered someone
Everyone just busted into laughter, with Musa standing there short for words.
Now you know the person called No steady and his unsteady character but one incident that has left an indelible impression on my mind whenever I think of him was a game at the snooker pool table.

We were all gathered round the snooker table brooding over our multiple loses from one guy brought by the boardman to quickly relief us of our contract in other to make more money.
'Anymore', the pro asked, 'it seems none of you has a strong hand?' Just then No steady strolled in.
'Don No steady, na you biko', all hailed him.
'Wetin dey celine dion? He asked

'No be celine dion, this one na busta rhyme' Jide answered, 'this guy has dealt with us hands down'.
'Its no problem, am around! Replied No steady ' Board man, come and rack the game'.
'where is your money"
'Why are you like this? I would settle you now! He answered
'There is never a day you come here with money, always talk and no action'.
'So you don't have money and you are behaving as if you would buy the board'. The pro inquired.
'Who is this? Somebody please play him my tape'
'No steady, No steady' rented the air.
'Please give him a game on me let me see his hand'. The pro requested
The game was racked, the pro went first, he broke and a ball entered a hole, he aimed at another ball, which to him would favour his shot, the ball simply missed its targeted pocket. No steady collected the Q stick, pots three balls before missing and passing to the pro, who potted all his balls remaining the black ball, he doubled and missed, No steady utilized his remaining two shots properly potting all his remaining balls including the black ball.
Everyone applauded No steady, shouts of No steady No steady rented the air.
'I told you, he would e beaten by me, he isn't my match'.

He boasted
'Look here, let me tell you, I dashed you that game'.
Defended the pro.
'Gist, you can't play me and you are talking about dashing me a game, I won clean clear'. He replied.
'Okay then, let's go betting', challenged the pro
'I don't have any money', replied No steady
'Drop your wrist watch and I would drop five hundred naira'.
'Okay by me' he replied already pulling his wristwatch.
The board man racked and the first shot was launched by No steady, two different balls entered different pockets, he chose the ball which favours him the most, one two into the pot, missed and hands over the Qstick to the pro, slow and straight shots, slow and cutting shots, potting four balls before missing a target. Collecting the Qstick with agility, No steady launched a one shot double hit, potting his remaining two balls and left with the black ball, he took aim, a straight shot, it entered and bounced out.
'What it did not enter', someone shouted
'Keep quite, don't you know they are betting', rebuked the board man.
'Damn it, that ball did not enter, then am finished'. No steady stated
Receiving the Qstick, the pro potted his last two balls, preparing to finish the game with the black ball.

'Just watch the ball go in', boasted the pro
No steady having already giving up, went to sit on the bench and thinking of his beloved wristwatch.
A hard shot was taken by the pro, maybe it was too hard or what but everyone was shocked because the ball entered the pot and bounced out, rolling just at the tip of the mouth of the pot.
'Ehwo, see what just happened', lamented the pro.
Jumping to his feet, No steady collected the Qstick took his aim and in the black ball went.
Everybody was jubilant, celebrating No steady.
'I told you, I told you I will deal with you', No steady was boasting
'That's nothing, lets go some more', replied the pro
'How much? Asked No steady
'One thousand naira', replied the pro
'I would drop the five hundred naira plus my wristwatch.
The game was racked.
'I will give you three balls' challenged the pro
'I will deal with you anyway', replied No steady
The pro launched the first shot, selecting three balls and placing in the pocket. The game became really calculative, every loose move means something, so shots were taken accurately with care. For every shot the pro took, if it doesn't favor him, he hides the white ball behind his ball, the game was going on smoothly with each potting almost all their balls, over confidence made

No steady lose a shot, capitalizing on this loss, the pro potted his remaining ball, leaving him with the decisive black ball which was being blocked by No steady's ball. He took a careful aim, released a doubling shot, reaching its destination, the ball touched the edge of the pocket, moving to the other side and spinning lazily and gently, holding the breath of everyone but finally dropping with a shout from everyone's mouth.
'I say, why e no go drop, eh, tell me, why e no go drop! The pro boasted, ' abeg, give me my money and watch make I waka'.
Everyone around for the first time where unified in grief with No steady over his loss. But I was not surprised to see No steady doing what he knows how to do best.
'Its nothing! He said following the pro.
I watched as they went away, No steady trying to convince the pro to return his wristwatch. I only shook my head departing.

(83)
WE FELL APART

After series of tribulation
A path to frustration
Mock adumbration
Misunderstood notion
Of motive; lead finally

We fell apart.

Supposed twined condition
A long awaited separation
A feeling of nostalgion.

Each having
Understanding
Why? You lack understanding
Can't we but be understanding
Having a little understanding
Applying nothing but understanding?
But finally we fell apart.

All to your tent
Like the twin kernel
Broken apart.
Hurting? noooo
Not feeling
Knowing not how to feel.
Now that
We fell apart.

(84)
RAINFALL
Cascading down verociously
In the sullen moment

Socket swollen opened
Peppered from enamoured display
Of sunken brief despair
"give me that tears and live on life's
Glorious annals".
Pitiful!

(85)
FUNK

My lady of pearl
You glow like the essence
That is you.
Radiant like the spraying
Rays of the moon.
Spreading like the bloom
At the start of hammathan
Brightening as sunny day.
My lady of pearl
You are the benevolence
Of my existence.

(86)
JUST YOU

I don't want a saint
But just you
Just you
To fill my inner recesses
With your fire.

Just you
To consume my being
With your fury.
Just you
To melt my essence
With your kisses.
Not a saint
But just you.

(87)
EARLY BLOOMER

We all blossom
After planting, watering,
Nurturing and culturing….
We all blossom into
Beautiful creations.

(88)
JUST THINKING

Must love be expressed
In words or through cards
Or through gifts
Or even still through
Flowers?
Must love be expressed
Under the starry skies
Or over lighted

Candled tables?
Cannot love
Just be known
When contacted
With this activities
That put unwholesome
Pressure on
This one purity.

(89)
FRIEND

I try to make a friend
But came to look like a fiend.
So am taken to defend
Which is this trend
Which is already confirmed
And cannot be constrained.

(90)
CYCLE

When the time is right
I would call on the powers
To come into my grief
And give me relief
From the life that I live
As it is my belief
That I can retrieve

Having no disbelief
My path to wealth,
Status
Prestige.

(91)
BLACK MEMORIAM

Need we shed tears
Before we smile?
Need we go to war
Before we have peace?
Need we reiterate the common
Before we get the basic?
Need we be damaged totally
Before succor come?   GOD
This second curse
I must break
I must destroy
I must crush
I must extinguish
My singular anguish
…..save me from this
Black cry…. Father.

(92)
DUMMY

Why? Haven't you learned the simple ways of

Building family relationship?
Why? Are you so far from reality?
Why? Is it so difficult, in being more sensitive
To the welfare conditions of your creations?
Why? Cant you display the Christian charity as
Exemplified by the carpenter's son?
Why? Are you and strive veritable partners?
One cannot think of you without the other
Like twin buds, going hand in hand.
Break out! Break out!
And live free! And live fulfilled.

(93)
BROKEN DAWN

My pain is confounded
Wanting a parting from
But more compounded….
Your strides
        Your vituperance
        Your insensitivity
        Your temperance
        Your rigidity.
Haven't you any resilence
Of time?

In my struggling hours and days, I thank the good LORD that I have my mum and was very much unattached.

(94)
THIS TIME

With the waking of dawn
A heaviness.
With the setting of the weather
A stiffness.
Doubting thomases beclouding
The glory of the rising sun
With its rays so bright
Formidable
And so invigorating.
With a commanding
Intrigue
I rise
Yes
I rise
And
I shine.

(95)
CIRCLE

I stand
On the hollowness of my making
I sought
With a stubbornness unparalled.
Upon my feet

To worship
All bestowing
Kicking aside as dust
Unbefitting my regal footing.
Such nyphm's
With undiluted candour.
My making
This aloneness now.

(96)
BLACK CYCLE

Intermittent break
Never enough
In breaking
This elongated chain
Clasping
All rat racers racing
In a bludgeon race
Of colour, band and beret
Consummate......
Is not the prirean pool
One's prerogative?

(97)
THE RUNWAY

My midnight partners

Wriggling to take position
In annihilating drunken
Anopheles landing
On netted runway.

11

Tossing from one end to another
Wringling from one corner to another
Two neighbours
Under the midnight moonlight
One is feed on
The other feed's on
One is suffocated
With the cymbatic acrobic
Of anophile's blood suckers
The other is intoxicated
With annihilating
Over drunken resting anopheles.

(98)
SMILE

When you see me
Flash your set thirty two.
However dull, however bright
When you see me.

When you see me

Form for me a rainbow
Beaming colours, shining armours
When you see me.

(99)
GODDESS

Let me keep watch
Over you grove image
And worship at your
Sacred shrine….. pouring
Spasm smoldered libation
All over
Your pearly smoothness
……beautiful…….

                                            Ii

Overwhelmed with rhapsodic
Dancing…..in calypsonic
Gyrating to the rhythm
Of sensual kinetic….

(100)
HOPE

Lets me take solace
In dreams yet accomplished.
Let me take refuge
In goals yet fulfilled.
As I apply faith
Waiting for the breaking

Of my kernel.

(101)
RESOLUTION

I have passed through hunger
I have passed through disappointment
I have passed through losses
I have passed through homelessness
I have passed through deprivation
But am not giving up.

I have passed through shame
I have passed through neglect
I have passed through heart breaks
I have passed through hopelessness
I have passed through pains
But am not giving up.

I have passed through failure
I have passed through oppression
I have passed through depression
I have passed through eventlessness
I have passed through confusion
But am not giving up

(102)
NOT AFRAID

Not afraid to fail in other to succeed

Not afraid to fall in other to rise
Not afraid to wait in other to get
Not afraid, no, not afraid to keep trying.

Not afraid to want in other to receive
Not afraid to seek in other to find
Not afraid to take a step in other to move forward.
Not afraid, no, not afraid to keep trying.

Not afraid to contend in other to overcome
Not afraid to do what it takes in other to get a change
Not afraid to take risks in other to know if I would succeed.
Not afraid, no, not afraid to keep trying.

Not afraid to encounter obstacles in other to believe everything would be okay
Not afraid to pray in other to have an answer
Not afraid to have faith in other to have the impossible
Not afraid, no, not afraid to keep trying.

Not afraid to embrace the mystery called everyday in other to get a miracle
Not afraid to lend a helping hand in other to save a soul
Not afraid to step out into the sunlight in other to be enveloped in its warmth.
Not afraid, no, not afraid to keep trying.

Not afraid to love in other to be loved
Not afraid to look you in the eyes in other to say I love you
Not afraid to pursue in other to win your heart
Not afraid to indulge in other to gain your trust
Not afraid to remain steadfast in other to have your hand in holy wedlock.
Not afraid, no, not afraid to keep trying.

Not afraid to shout aloud in other to be relieved
Not afraid to scream in other to be heard
Not afraid to move mountains in other to get to my destination.
Not afraid, no, not afraid to keep trying.

(103)
WELCOME

She sits still
Smiling sporaciously
At all and sundry
Trying to make
Their day!
A soliciting to comeback.
But alas…..who is making
Her day…..smily?

WISE SAYINGS/QUOTABLE QUOTES OF MINE AND OTHERS

(1)What can a man hope for if not for better days. Can man truly be careful? - Stephen Orukpe Esq

(2)Do that which you believe in most, never work with the mouth of men, or else you fall. For only time would bail you out.-Stephen Orukpe Esq

(3)Only time bears the fruit of our actions and inactions.- Stephen Orukpe Esq

(4)Never say you cannot be deceived by a woman; a woman trick is innumerable. For a woman who knows her worth is worth her salt.- Stephen Orukpe Esq

(5)Never be excessively filled with laughter or else you become foolish.- Stephen Orukpe Esq

(6)It is very hard following a failed and struggling man, however wise he may seem. - Stephen Orukpe Esq

(7)A failed man always looks for scape goats.- Stephen Orukpe Esq

(8)You walk straight into a ditch and you say 'I was chased' but were you blind?.- Stephen Orukpe Esq

(9)Everything we do begin from the inside, look inward to get a better scape goat and you would be at peace with men.- Stephen Orukpe Esq

(10)Avoidance is the best way when been suspicious; cutting off when confirmed, those who seeks your mortal hurt.- Stephen Orukpe Esq

(11) Looking inward is the best way of solving ones problems. Seek counsel from those advance than you but never you go near one who is a fool.- Stephen Orukpe Esq

(12) Do what you know is right even if all odds are against you. Time will bear you out. - Stephen Orukpe Esq

(13) It has never been the money, because money will always follow a successful endeavour, it has always been about just doing it. That you can beat your chest and say, it was I who did that and it succeeded.- Stephen Orukpe Esq

(14) Loyalty is dedication and slavery; disloyalty independence.- Stephen Orukpe Esq

(15) To say you have is good but to truly have is better. endeavor to always have.- Stephen Orukpe Esq

(16) Satisfaction comes from having that which you are contented with.- Stephen Orukpe Esq

(17) To place ones hope on people is the most dangerous of all vices. it is like building ones house of sandy soil.- Stephen Orukpe Esq

(18) He does not want to help you, if he is looking for words from your mouth to use against you.- Stephen Orukpe Esq

(19) It is the believing which does the working.- Stephen Orukpe Esq

(20) Build your life upon a solid foundation and be able to control that which you have built before you can truly be

able to reachout to others.- Stephen Orukpe Esq
(21)Be patience and at all times be reasonable with he who never sees your line of reasoning.- Stephen Orukpe Esq
(22)Love is the twin brother of hate.- Stephen Orukpe Esq
(23)The sweetness of having power is so intoxicating that it urges on the will and desire of wanting more.- Stephen Orukpe Esq
(24)Beginning is one thing, continuing another, getting to the final peak, something totally different altogether.- Stephen Orukpe Esq
(25)Man is an active machine, to undermine one is losing a potential tool in the machinery.- Stephen Orukpe Esq
(26)Any activity which gets to the stage of being out of control is bad.- Stephen Orukpe Esq
(27)Never be overcome by the disadvantages but think always of the advantages.- Stephen Orukpe Esq
(28)Self determination makes the seem impossible possible.Never occupy, always be occupied.- Stephen Orukpe Esq
(29)To be successful is in no way indicative of an automatic atmost magical immunity to insecurity, pain, loss, depression, despondency, death, authority and all imaginable laws regular people are prone to.- Anonymous
(30)The totality of a good story takes into account a good theme, good plotting and well developed characters, a good visual creation must conform to the essence of high

art that marries ideas with beauty- Anonymous

(31) What is meaning? Is meaning entirely dependent on known fact and if so in a case of the limited knowledge of fact, how definite, reliable and authentic can meaning be?- Anonymous

(32) Good and honest communication is always the key to positive relationships that sustain effective functioning of the entire system.- Anonymous

(33) Let me do today that which I wouldn't regret not doing tomorrow, so whenever I look back, a full smile of contentment would spring on my face.- Stephen Orukpe Esq

(34) The price of excellence is consistency of purpose and discipline.- Stephen Orukpe Esq

(35) Born to do great things; you aint seen the best of this son of man; born to achieve great things.- Stephen Orukpe Esq

Conceptualise; actualize; be rooted; I am stabilized for business.- Stephen Orukpe Esq

(36) Always know your time and place.- Stephen Orukpe Esq

(37) Everything is dual, everything has poles, everything has its pair of opposite, like and unlike are the same, opposite are identical in nature, but different in decree, extreme meet, all truth are half truths, all paradoxes may be reconciled.- Anonymous

(38) Everything flows out and in, everything has its roles,

all things rise and fall, the pendulum swing manifest in everything; the measure of the swing to the right is the measure to the left; rhythm compensates.- Anonymous
(39) Every cause has its effect, every effect has its cause, everything happens according to law, chance is a name for law unrecognized; there are many planes of causation, but nothing escapes the law.-Anonymous
(40) As soon as man is moving with the current, all he has to do is let himself go; with no trouble he can make an immense fortune.- Anonymous
(41) Happiness does not lie in vanity, it only brings regrets, sorrow, depression. Learn to live in your present and face your reality with honor, cut down excesses, calling always on God to guide and strengthen you! Be wise.- Stephen Orukpe Esq
(42) Know that a little light dispenses darkness.- Stephen Orukpe Esq
(43) Be a man of authority- always recognize the power of the positive force.- Stephen Orukpe Esq
(44) Always be confident; never allow despair find a resting place in you.- Stephen Orukpe Esq
(45) It is impossible to be cheated out of an honourable career unless one cheats himself.- Stephen Orukpe Esq
(46) Recognize your moment of lifting up.- Stephen Orukpe Esq
(47) Know that your steps matters a lot.- Stephen Orukpe Esq

(48) Know that you are a multitudinous individual.- Stephen Orukpe Esq
(49) Know that there exist powers and there exist powers.- Stephen Orukpe Esq
(50) Know that truth not recognized does not work.- Stephen Orukpe Esq
(51) Know it has happened.- Stephen Orukpe Esq
(52) A lot of times before every great fortune, there is a crime- Don Corleone (The Godfather)
(53) Never negate the power of contact-Don Corleone Society imposes insults that must be borne and also there comes a time when the most humble of men, if he keeps his eyes open, can take his revenge on the most powerful- Don Corleone
(54) Always put intruders out of your mind while at work.-Don Corleone
(55) Make it a point of duty to profit from everything.- Don Corleone
(56) Know when to be notoriously straitlaced.-Don Corleone
(57) Show your generosity as personal-Don Corleone
(58) Do not spun reasonable friendship.-Don Corleone
(59) Know that this world is not a harmless place where you could take your pleasure as you willed.-Don Corleone
(60) Arm yourself with true friends-Don Corleone
(61) Never thrust your friendship on those who do not value it, on those who think you of little account-Don

Corleone

(62) Be forceful and voiceful.-Don Corleone

(63) Life is full of misfortunes.-Don Corleone

(64) Prepare to give an eye for an eye.-Don Corleone

(65) Reliability is acceptability; know how to be a father to your children, then you are a real man.-Don Corleone

(66) Never allow women dictate your actions- Don Corleone

(67) Friendship is more than talent, it is more than government, it is everything, almost equal to the family.-Don Corleone

(68) Build a solid wall of friendship and always look out for reasonable men, for with them problems of business could always be solved.-Don Corleone

(69) Make an offer they won't refuse and make it an affair of personal honor-Don Corleone

(70) Let your word count; be organized.-Don Corleone

(71) The use of threat is the most foolish kind of exposure; the most dangerous indulgence is anger without fore thought.-Don Corleone

(72) Never show your true self, for after midnight, morning would come.-Don Corleone

(73) Any profession is worthy of respect to men who earned their bread by the sweat of their brows.-Don Corleone

(74) Time would heal wounds; pain and terror were not so final as death.-Don Corleone

(75) Time erodes gratitude more quickly than it does beauty.-Don Corleone
(76) No matter the number of mistakes we make, it is the lesson derived thereof that matters.-Don Corleone
(77) Peace is not only the absence of tension but the presence of justice.-Don Corleone
(78) Make your meaning clear and understanding and learn to address issues more appropriately; never brood over grudges.-Don Corleone
(79) Be polite and reasonable; never lose focus and be manipulative.-Don Corleone
(80) Sometimes the greatest misfortune brought unforeseen rewards.-Don Corleone
(81) Attitude determine action; action determine your accomplishment-Don Corleone
(82) Women and children can afford to be careless; men cannot and everyman should be allowed one foolishness in his life.-Don Corleone
(83) Always have them puzzled.-Don Corleone
(84) Build your family to be loyal so as to be trusted than society and keep your mind in tact; there lies your strength.- Don Corleone
(85) Live in your reality, never despair and mothers are like cops, they always believe the worst.-Don Corleone
(86) Society doesn't really protect its members who do not have their own individual power and a friend should always underestimate your virtue and an enemy over

estimate your faults.-Don Corleone

(87) Life is beautiful and revenge is a dish well served when it is cold-Don Corleone

(88) Prudence, be prudent and be full of nobility and dignity, believe in yourself and nothing else would matter.-Don Corleone

(89) Don't rush at provocation, sometimes it is better to sit and watch, never get angry, never make a threat, reason with people, never be too open mouthed ask for information, however little, however small and always

(90) know what you are up against.-Don Corleone

(91) Conscience does make coward of us all.-Don Corleone

(92) The profile of a wealthy man is this: hardwork-perserverance-self discipline; be persistent, consistent, disciplined and hard working.-Don Corleone

(93) Genius has its rewards; make the other party superstitious; never be hasty to speech, be considerate and never be too excited among strangers.-Don Corleone

(94) Make it known, for nobody outside the family should know what you are thinking and doing.-Don Corleone

(95) Never let them know what you have under your fingernails; read through me, know your opponent and see through him.-Don Corleone

(96) Don't be foolish, never get into something you would lose more rather than gain and only allow one word against another, not two against one.-Don Corleone

(97) Always be mysterious and extremity sometimes pays.-Don Corleone
(98) Never underestimate the power of money changing hands.-Don Corleone
(99) Fish out early the little foxes that would spoil the vine.-Bible
(100) There is a difference between security and guns.-Don Corleone
(101) Every business of your life, take it personal and find your path and walk it to success.- Don Corleone
(102) Take your time, allow your feelings to be deep-rooted; there lies your strength and never show what you are thinking.-Don Corleone
(103) A decision at a point would change the entire cause of ones life; so watch what decisions you make and it is not the time one begins but how one begins, start with a florish.-Don Corleone
(104) Be not limited in your sense of judgment and opportunity, know your words.-Don Corleone
(105) Be sincerely charitable and never show your greed rather be guided by it.-Don Corleone
(106) Always have your sense of reasoning, be a man of respect; great men are not usually born great, they grow great.-Don Corleone
(107) Never underestimate the power of contact, knowledge, opportunity and experience and always have some self interest with your generosity.- Don Corleone

(108) I only wanted to build an economic and political empire but lady luck never took a fancy towards me. As I continue to bear my root curse.- Stephen Orukpe Esq

(109) Never look at your opponent size, focus on your organizational strength.- Stephen Orukpe Esq

(110) Plan for the future, have fore sight; the present is nothing but a stepping stone.- Stephen Orukpe Esq

(111) The bee that makes the honey does not hang around the hive.- Anonymous

(112) The road to failure is greased with the slime of indifference.-Anonymous

(113) Some carve out a future, while others just whittle away the time. Anonymous

(114) Never has a man who lives a life of ease, left a name worth remembering.-Anonymous

(115) Most of our troubles arise from loafing when we should be working.- Anonymous

(116) No one has ever climbed a hill by just looking at it.- Anonymous

(117) If the devil catch a man idle, he will set him at work.- Anonymous

(118) Just over the hill is a beautiful valley but you must climb the hill to see it.- Anonymous

(119) Ambition never gets anywhere until it forms partnership with work- Anonymous

(120) No dream comes true until you wake up and go to work.-Anonymous

(121) Moved by deep love, a man is courageous and with frugality a man becomes generous. And he who does not desire to be ahead of the world becomes the leader of the world- The natural way of law- Tzu

(122) The secret of success is sweat and one thing that keeps a lot of people from being a success is work.- Anonymous

(123) Faith may move mountains but only hard work and smart work can put a tunnel through.- Anonymous

(124) Men who earn true respect are those who know when to draw the line.-Anonymous

(125) Winning is not a sometime thing, it is an all the time thing, you don't win once in a while, you don't do things right once in a while, you do them right all the time- Vince Lombardi

(126) The probability that we may fail does not deter us from the pursuit of a great and noble cause we believe is just.- Abraham Lincoln

(127) The soul of a man endlessly or perpetually search for fame thus lofty soul is interested in little and unworthy things.-Max Engel

(128) The ultimate worth of a man is not measured in times of comfort and happiness but it is measured in time of trials and challenges.-Theodore Roosevelt

(129) Am not a failure; I would not accept failure. In accepting one failure, you accept another, then another until it becomes a trend and finally you are out. I stand

only for success.
(130) Ever do men mistake guilt for dignity and lies for truth.- Anonymous
(131) Fortune sometimes favors fools.-Anonymous
(132) The world is a jungle and a man has only two choices either to be a tiger or a jackal.-Anonymous
(133) Pride makes a lean belly.- Anonymous
(134) The eyes are the mirror of a man's soul.- Anonymous
(135) Happiness, I fear and distrust it. The fates permit it to a man only to make his subsequent suffering the keener.- Oedisus- Iliad
(136) Our expectation has a great deal to do with our attitude.- Pastor Taiwo Odukoya
(137) Ability is what you are capable of doing, motivation determines what you do. Attitude will determine how well you do it.-Anonymous
(138) Your attitude would determine your altitude- Lou Horz
(139) Words can never adequately convey the incredible impact of our attitude toward life.- Anonymous
(140) The longer I live, the more convinced I become that life is 10% of what happens to us and 90% of how we respond to it- Swindoll
(141) It is our inability to prevent and control change that has brought about the termination of many dreams and dashing many hopes.- Pastor Taiwo Odukoya

(142) The way you depart your last stage of life determines how you enter or begin the next.-Pastor Taiwo Odukoya

(143) True heroism is remarkably sober….it is not the urge to surpass all others at whatever cost but the urge to serve others at whatever cost.-Arthur Ashe

(144) Celebrated heroes have been able to identify their time and location to manifest heroism.- Anonymous

(145) Timing is the essential ingredient to success: being the right man at the right time in the right place. The right sequence is vital.-Edwin Louis Cole

(146) Many are waiting to be liberated, many are waiting to be elevated, many are waiting to be inspired. It is time to confront and conquer. This is just your time.-Anonymous

(147) If a man hasn't discovered something that he will die for, he isn't fit to live.- Martin Luther

(148) Justice is a man made word. We are but the sports of chance, the creature of blind accidentality; the play thing of mocking ribald gods who love us not. Our faith is a sentimental thing, hardly justified by the slightest evidence of our eyes.-Anonymous

(149) Nothing is impossible; there are ways that lead to everything, and if we had sufficient will, we should always have sufficient means. It is often merely for an excuse that we say things are impossible.- Francois La Rochefoucald

(150) I know of no more encouraging fact than the unquestionable ability of man to elevate his life by a conscious endeavor.-Henry David Thoreau

(151) Two men look out through the same prison bars; one sees the mud and the other sees the stars.- Frederick Kangbridge

(152) Impossibility is only a state of mind; most times, it is merely someone's opinion imposed on you.- Anonymous

(153) The oppositions before you and the challenges around you are insignificant in comparison to our actual possibilities.-Anonymous

(154) Until you stretch yourself, you can never know what you are capable of.- Anonymous

(156) A man's mind, stretched by a new idea, can never go back to its original dimension.-Oliver Wendell Holmes.

(157) A man who knows what he wants and knows that it is possible and is determined to pay the price to get it, no matter what, is a dangerous man. Don't even try to stand in his way.- Anonymous

(158) Its not the critics who counts. Its not the man who points out the strong man stumble, or where the doer of the deed could have done it better. The credit belongs to those who are actually in the arena, who strive valiantly; who knows the great enthusiaims, the great devotion and spend themselves in a worthy cause; who at the best knows the triumph of high achievements and who at the

worst, if they fail, fail while daring greatly. So that their place shall never be with those cold and timid souls who know neither victory nor defeat.- Theodore Roosevelt

(159) I am enough of an artist to draw freely upon my imagination. Imagination is more important than knowledge; knowledge is limited. Imagination encircles the world.-Albert Einstein

(160) We use our imagination to chart the course of our future. We use our imagination to determine the direction of our lives. In our imagination, we create our worlds.-Anonymous

(161) Dream big dreams! Others may deprive you of your material wealth and cheat you in a thousand way, but no man can deprive you of the control and use of your imagination. Men may deal with you unfairly as men often do, they may deprive you of your rights and priviledges, but they can't take from you the priviledge of using your imagination. For in your imagination, you will always win.-Jesse Jackson

(162) Set out each day believing in your dreams. Know without doubt that you were made for amazing things. Understand that it is okay to be scared or uncertain, however right beyond those barriers ultimately lies your dreams.- Josh Hinds

(163) If one advances confidently in the direction of their dreams, and endeavor to lead a life which they have imagined, they will meet a success unexpected in

common hours.-Henry David Thoreau

(164) If you can see it in your mind, you can achieve it; if you can see it in your mind, you can have it; if you can imagine it, then it is possible.-Anonymous

(165) To make your life small when it can be great is a sin and an heresy.-Elton Trueblood

(166) Everyman's work, whether it be literature or music or pictures or architecture or anything else is always a portrait of himself.-Samuel Butler

(167) Nobody really fails until they accept failure as a finality.- Anonymous

(168) If you can control a man's thought, ypu do not have to worry about his actions, when you determine what a man shall think, you do not have to concern yourself about what he will do; if you make a man feel he s inferior, you do not have to compel him to seek an inferior status, for he will seek it himself; if you make a man feel that he is justly an outcast, you do not have to order him to the back door, he will go without being told; and if there is no backdoor, his very nature will demand one.-Carter G. Woodson

(169) Our actions will always be consistent with whatever we think of ourselves.-Anonymous

(170) Self-respect is the noblest garment with which a man may clothe himself. The most elevating feeling with which the mind can be inspired.-Anonymous

(171) I find that great things in this world is not so much

where we stand, as in what direction we are moving: to reach the port of heaven, we must first sail sometimes with the wind and sometimes against it-but we must sail and not drift, nor lies at anchor.- Oliver Wendell Holmes
(172) Fight one more round. When your arms are so tired that you can hardly lift your hands to come on guard, fight one more round. When your nose is bleeding and
(173) your eyes black and you are so tired that you wish your opponent would crack you one the jaw and put you to sleep. Fight one more round remembering that the man who always fights one more round is never whipped.-James Corbelt
(174) Nothing can resist a human will that will stake even its very existence on his stated purpose.-Benjamin Disrael
(175) If I see what I want real good, I don't notice any pain getting it.-George Foreman
(176) He who has a why to live for can bear almost anyhow.- Friedrich Nietzsche
(177) I have learned over the years that when one's mind is made up, this diminishes fear; knowing what must be done does away with fear.-Rosa Parks
(178) A man may fall many times but he won't be a failure until he says someone pushed him.-Elmer G. Letterman
(179) Don't go around saying the world owes you a living; the world owes you nothing; it was here first.- Mark Twain
(180) When the archer misses the mark, he turns and

looks for the fault within himself. Failure to hit the bulls eyes is never the fault of the target. To improve your target, improve yourself.-Gilbert Arland

(181) People are always blaming their circumstances for what they are. I don't believe in circumstances. The people who get on in this world are the people who get up and look for the circumstances they want and if they can't find them, make them.- George Shaw

(182) All blame is a waste of time. No matter how much fault you find with another and regardless of how much you blame that another, it will not change you. The only thing blame does is to keep the focus off you when you are looking for external reasons to explain your unhappiness or frustration. You may succeed in making another feel guilty about something by blaming him, but you won't succeed in changing whatever it is about you that is making you unhappy.-Wayne Dyer

(183) Unless you attempt to do something beyond that which you have already mastered, you will never grow.-Anonymous

(184) If a man empties his purse into his head, no man can take it away from him- An investment in knowledge always pays the best interest.-Benjamin Franklin

(185) If a man can write a better book, preach a better sermon or make a better mouse trap than his neighbor, though he builds his house in the woods, the world will make a beaten path to his doors.- Emerson

(186) The quality of a person's life is in direct proportion to his/her commitment to excellence, regardless of the chosen field of endeavor.- Vincent T. Lombardi
(187) I studied the lives of great men and famous women, and I found that men and women who got to the top were those who did the jobs they had in hand, with everything they had of energy and enthusiasm and hardwork.- Harry S. Truman
(188) God gave us the nuts but he didn't crack them- German Proverbs
(189) My philosophy is that not only are you responsible for your life, but he best at the moment puts you in the best place for the next moment.- Oprah Winfrey
(190) A year from today, you will remain the same person you are today, except for the people you meet and the books you read.-Charles 'Tremendous' Jones
(191) Be a jack of many trade for you don't have to be a master of all but you must make money from all.- Stephen Orukpe Esq

104.
WEDDING THINGS

I want to wed today
To put on my best designers suit
And see my bride look like Cinderella.
Walking to the altar
To the rhythm of an acapella.

I want to wed today
And hear the minister say
"for this reason shall a man
Leave his father and mother
And be joined to his wife".

I want to wed today
Having obtained favour from God
To find a wife, which is the good thing
A till death do us parting.

105
THONG THINGS

Am a man with the ring
And have many sides fling.
My number one has a boy
But her puny gives me joy.
Number two is of the moon and crescent
Oh gosh her moan so pubescent.
Three is only available in the morning
I make out time cos of her loud moaning.
Four just tell her money
She will meet you anywhere with her honey.
My five likes to jive
Before letting you in to dive.
Oh six is my sweet sixteen doll
With her nothing is dull.
Seven is a university student
In bed I take lectures as her student.
Eight very much likes mouthing
Sixty-nine being her thing.
Crazy nine likes it in her twos hole

I delight her with my long pole.
Delectable ten is my lepa shandy
Who is crazy for my sugar candy.
Eleven with her rotund behind
Bending her to enter like it is divined.
12, 13, 14, 15 and so on
I can't resist it, so I go on and on.

106
IF I BE A POET THAT

If I be a poet that
Is called to presidential inauguration
To rhyme my rhythm to a standing ovation.

If I be a poet that
Gets various corporate endorsement
My bank account fills me with excitement.

If I be a poet that
Easily can afford the latest benz
Cruising on the high way dense.

If I be a poet that
Easily flies around the globe
Collaborating with other poets which is so dope.

If I be a poet that
Is not only creative
But is also innovative.

If I be a poet that
Is all about being innovative
Cause making money my motive.

If I be a poet that
Can churn out a sound laced CD of poetry
Hearing it in cars, clubs, radio, television, my solo entry.

If I be a poet that
Will get the accolade of a contemporary musician
As I bard along being a body and soul physician.

If I be a poet that
Can foot my basic bills
Even as I confront societal ills

If I be a poet that...

SHORT STORY FIVE

HAPPY NEW YEAR

i
HAPPY TIMES

One of my favorites moments is new-year's eve, it is the best time of the year not because the house is usually full with relatives or that your normal morning chores now has sufficient hands to handle it or the preparation and going for watch night service, afterwards the freedom to blow knock-outs and fire crackers from church till we get home or that the house remains open all night because there seems to be an endless activities going on which leads into the morning when the ram Baba bought will be slaughtered.
Nothing thrills me more than knowing I would be assigned the entrails of the ram for washing and cleaning afterwards to be used for pepper soup.
I had hardly slept on my mat when a rough hand shook me, opening my eyes, of course it was my cousin Omonigho, my pleasured tormentor.
"What now, why won't you allow me sleep" I screamed with all my body still full of sleep, being that I was in sweet thoughts most part of the night leading to new-year's eve.
"Wake up, lazy boy and hope you have not wet the floor? Pisi pisi! She questioned.
Immediately my hands went to my pants to investigate the obvious, thank God, I didn't pee on myself this time around.

"Mama wants you to go clean the place where the ram was tied and kept as well as feed it now", She said, storming out of the room.
I gradually got up, sleep leaving my body already and my mind regaining alertness to the assignment set before me as I woke my two younger brothers up to prepare them for bathing, brushing their tooth and changing their clothes before breakfast.
"Good morning brother, good morning Sister, Uncle good morning, Aunty good morning", I greeted here and there.
"Ah, good morning ojare and how are you" replied Mama Titi hurrying to the kitchen.
General greetings could be heard all around as I went to get my toothbrush to brush my teeth and then set out to the pen where the ram was kept to clean its feaces and feed it its marsh.
Outside, I saw Baba having his head shaved by that Mallam who usually come every end of month to shave and dye his hair; ducking my head so he wouldn't see me, I quickly brushed my teeth, drank some fresh water and ran inside, of course I would go over to greet him once he is through with the dyeing and shaving ritual.
"Bishop are you still playing around, have you gone to clear the ram's pen and fed it as well as replacing its water this morning"?, screamed Sister Nene.
Ducking my head inside, I ran over to where the pen was located at the back of our compound after rushing to greet my dad and mum, handling a broom and dust pan, I set for my morning duty. I swept away the dried faeces and filled the water can with water as well as its marsh.

Across from where I was, my several aunties where gathered round the several tubers of yams and cassava heaped, preparing for the next day being new year, with the main menu being pounded yam, ogbono soup and black soup. While at it, they are also busy preparing for the morning breakfast which is tea and bread.
Mama was not among them, of course, she would be in her room holding council with most of the women from our community, listening and giving advice to their numerous family complaints.

(pisi pisi means one who wets themselves at night)(ojare is a resigned acceptance of greetings by the yoruba's in Nigeria, West Africa) (Ogbono is a local soup of mostly Esan people of Edo State in Nigeria, West Africa)

ii
BIRTHDAY PARTY

Having concluded my assignment and seeing my usual morning chore of sweeping the compound has been effectively and dutifully carried out by one of my visiting cousins, am left with nothing doing for the main time other than waiting for my breakfast or go have my bath and ensure my siblings do same too.
Like it was yesterday, the year is suddenly coming to an end or what am I saying, today is the end of the year, whoa!
How times flies, when you least expected it. When was it

that one of my younger siblings had her birthday party?

The mood on that day was vivacious, gaiety, fun filled with laughter and joy. Felicia will be ten and a birthday was being put together by our dad and mom who wanted to celebrate her new age.
My younger sister seems lucky with celebrations, maybe because she always comes first in class and winning most of the prizes.
I cannot remember when my birthday was celebrated and am already thirteen and in secondary school. Well that didn't dampen my enthusiasm to enjoy myself and use her party to score points against most of our neighbors who have offended me.
On the day of Felicia's birthday, balloons decorations both in the sitting room and the car park area with rented white chairs already set and in the middle at the head of the front chairs was a single table meant for the cake.
Already, music has started blaring from the juke box of the DJ, hired for the event.
"Have you had your bath, eh Bishop", My Mum enquired.
"No Ma"
"Hurry and go have your bath, is it everything you will be reminded or told and where is Joshua and Caleb? Make sure they are ready too".
Her screams, sometimes blocking my ears, I just rushed to the bathroom and pushing the door.
"Ah ah, can't you knock", Felicia screamed
"I didn't know you were in there and don't be rude, simply because its your day today"

"Just close the door and come back when am finished"

As I shut the door, I heard her also say "and you haven't yet wished me happy birthday".
"Happy birthday" I shouted and went back to the sitting room brooding.
By now guest have started arriving and already my cousin and pleasured tormentor Omonigho was around.
"Jesus, you haven't yet dressed or what are you waiting for", Omonigho queried
"Look, just leave me alone oh, you hear" I scowled at her.
"Common it's a joyous day, be happy and put on a smile", she teased me playfully and I didn't realize when I ended up giggling and eventually laughing.
Then I saw some of our neighbors I had targeted and don't want to come for the party.
Tunde and Lukman and their younger ones, all cutely dressed had been invited by my parents, but I don't like especially Tunde and Lukman, they sometimes ago connived and had my bird cage destroyed and allowed my turtle dove to escape. I am still bitter about it.
I rushed out to confront both of them and to turn them back.
"Look here both of you, who invited you to our party ", I spoke angrily to both Tunde and Lukman.
"Your mum invited us" both replied
"Well I didn't invite you, so turn your back now and leave our compound".
"What are you doing, Bishop" Omonigho inquired, continuing "You don't be rude to guest especially when they were properly invited", She told me scoldingly.

I ignored her and was about to shove them forcefully out of our compound, when Baba called on me.

"Sir, am coming", I answered
As I rushed to answer his call, I looked back and saw Omonigho talking to both of them and leading them into the sitting area where chairs were arranged for guests.
I finished attending to Baba and had to go have my bath and also bath my other younger siblings, finished, got us all dressed and sauntered into the birthday proper which has kick-started.
I forgot about Tunde and Lukman and became involved with the party activities. My most exciting moment was during the games which I have been anticipating to participate in and win a set of water colors which was set for one of the games.
Time for the game, I volunteered likewise Tunde and Lukman. The game was simple, chairs were put in the middle and participants were to go round and round and when the music stops, you are to sit on any available chair, who doesn't have a chair to sit on, will be eliminated.
I was successful until it remained myself and Lukman going round a single chair, of course when the music stopped, I was the one who sat on the only chair and won the game as well as the price of the wrapped water color.
 This win gave me some measure of respite from the anger I felt for those duo.

INTEGRATED SCIENCE (BASIC SCIENCE)

Another interesting but sad aspect of the year happened to be resuming for a new semester at the beginning of the year now ending.

In one of the classes, the subject integrated science (basic science) was the topic of the hour. Our teacher, Mr Ade, standing in front of the class with his bespectacled face, wrote on the board INTEGRATED SCIENCE (BASIC SCIENCE).

"Now class, welcome back and down to business, before I introduce today's topic "BODY PARTS", who can recap for me the meaning of integrated science" asking the general class.

I ducked my head, not wanting to draw attention to myself while thinking, what is integrated science again. Then I heard my name!

"Bishop, do please be kind to recap for us the meaning of "Integrated Science"", I heard Mr Ade say.

Gosh, why me? and why now? Raising my head slowly and trying to stand up, Titi (oh blessed Titi) jumped to her feet and to my rescue and recapped the meaning of integrated science as an approach to teaching of all areas of science using an holistic approach in learning its basic principles.

"Well I actually didn't beckon on you but nonetheless, yes that is it class, she is correct, now to today's topic "BODY PARTS".

Both of us shared a pleasant look, with mine saying "Thank You", beaming with cheerfulness, she seem to say "you are welcome".

Mr Ade continued the teaching on the various body parts of both the male and female, already it was informative, exciting, confusing and discomforting.

You could hear giggles here and there from both the male and female students. Everytime, I sneak to take a look at Titi, she always catches my sneak look with lighted misty eyes. I became even more confused and uncomfortable.
Though she stays two streets from me and occasionally we o home together but normally, after school, she would go meet her mother at Mile 2 market to help out with sale of women materials and accessories being that her mother is a trader dealing in laces and other female wears.
I tried to avoid her during break time and even after close of school but was surprised she flound me and suggested I accompany her home.
"Thanks for rescuing me earlier", I said
'Oh its nothing, I knew immediately you were called that you were not ready for the recap", She giggled
"Don't mind teacher Ade, after all the celebration and the holidaying, how does he expect me to still remember meaning of integrated science" I scowled.
"Let's leave it, next time read your books even during holidays sometimes and not only play, play all day long", She scolded
We moved on to talking other things, reminding ourselves of something that happened in the past, laughed, giggled and quite unlike Titi, holding my hands now and again.
We got to her house and being alone, she told me to wait for her while she changed.
I sat on the sofa in the sitting room, looking and re-looking at all the framed photo pictures of her family lined on the wall when I felt a hand wrap my eyes, I jerked away and

turning, I saw Titi wrapped in a towel covering her upper and lower part with her hands and legs visible to the eyes.
"I want to show you my body part and I also want see your body part" She told me
Before I would protest, she let loose her towel, and I saw her full anatomy as described in class earlier, with my eyes bulging and hearing me gulp my saliva, I didn't hesitate to grab at my bag and dashed to the door and fled.
That whole day I wasn't myself and the next day, I avoided her. The following week, our teachers went on strike which lasted four weeks, after calling it off and resuming back to school, I noticed Titi didn't resume back to school with us. She sent a note through her friend Shola to inform me that she has changed school to a private boarding school in illesha, Osun State and that I should grow up.
Three months after, there was a nationwide as well as a worldwide lockdown due to corona virus pandemic.
After the ease of the lockdown and adhering to safety protocols like washing of hands and use of sanitizer, sneezing into ones elbow in public and use of face mask as well as social distancing were schools allowed to resume. Though the Lagos State government tried to use radio and television to teach students/pupils at home but it was not effective due to incessant power outage.
However, when things began to normalize and students were fully back to school that I got the shock and saddest news of the year; my Titi was dead from either corona virus complications or human immunodeficiency virus (HIV) or acquired immunodeficiency syndrome(AIDS). That in school she developed high fever and was rushed to the sick bay, were it was diagnosed that she has shortage of blood

and was giving blood transfusion which is one of the ways of contacting the disease likewise use of unsterilized needles, razor blade and unprotected sex. Getting home during the lockdown, her condition suddenly peaked and it ended in her death.

iv
RAIN, RAIN

The rainy season usually peaks in June, July and August. I live in our family compound with my grand dad, grand mom, father, mother, younger sister and brothers and tenants.

About four families make up our tenants and have children of same age, who happens to be our peers. We fight, quarrel, settle, share things and indulge in mischief together.

One of the most binding aspect of our collective and communal stay together was during the raining season. When the clouds become darken and wind changes its tune, all running helter-skelter with shouts, calling of names, carrying of valuables and running to safety as ones legs would.

Once the rains begins, the heavy down pour sends excitement down our spine, especially when we are back from school, during weekends or on holidays, all would rush out into the rain naked or on pants to bathe and splash cupped water at each other.

The heavy downpour backed by heavy winds increases the excitement. Everywhere, screams, shouts, so thrilling and exciting, feelings of joy. While boys of age set stones on the streets to play football.

"Monkey post, monkey post", I jumped into the arena of where the football is about to be played

"Will, you disappear from here, or is any of your mates here", Bros Niyi shouted angrily

"Bros, please na, I just want to play",

"Get out before they break your leg", He said, pushing my head.

Immediately, I recalled two episodes, one involving my younger brother whom sometime last year, I had rush to go call, only for him as he was rushing to go attend to the assignment he was called for, had an accident.

"Someone has been hit by a car" someone came to the field to inform everyone. Immediately we all rush to the scene, only to discover it was my younger brother in the ditch, the driver immediately picked him up, put him in his car and drove off.

Different stories were flying here and there, search to various places, hospitals, morgue, police stations, I have never been so scared in my life cause I was the one who went to call him.

"When they tell you to stay in one place, no, now look what has happened", Sister Nene was screaming angrily and at the same time slapping me with her both hands. My father just stood there watching speechless, while my mum was inside surrounded by relatives.

I just left everyone, went into the bedroom and prayed to God to bring him back and I will never play football again. By 7pm that same day, the driver came back with him to the street and was making inquires and was led to our compound, with shouts of jubilation, praise the lord, sign of relieve everywhere.

The second episode involved Uduak, who went to play football with some senior boys and got his leg broken. He had to be taken to his village and when he returned, though better, he still went around with a limp.

I gave up trying to join in the football game and ran inside the compound to join the others playing in the rain.

After my episode with Titi and her demise, I was no more, in honour of her memory, shy or perplexed again with the female anatomy.

No more curious in the sense that most of our female peers were already growing chest and it was no more unusually.

We now jovially tease our female peers and pinch at their growing chest. This is frequent especially during raining season public bath.

"See your pin pin", I pinched at the chest of Adanne

"Leave me oh, I will report you to brother kuku ooo, eh eh", Adanne will reply

Back and forth until we playfully will retire into our various apartments to dry and sleep soundly.

Already thirteen and still unspoiled or corrupted by the vagaries of life and its exigencies.

We lived life without complications and where more concerned about respect for our seniors, duties to our household, minor mischief here and there and as much as possible attending to our studies.

Playing in the rain naked with my female neighbors did not unblemished my innocence or corrupt my curiosity.

(pin pin for breasts)

V
HAPPY NEW YEAR

Seeing the house is full, myself and siblings as well as our neighbors children will from Christmas eve prepare a "Promise Me" list, where we have listed various items we carry around to various uncles and aunties, cajoling them to tick an item on the list as a promise to be fulfilled immediately or on or before new-year.

On new year's eve, we usually dust our "Promise Me" list and begin following up on those promises that are yet to be fulfilled and when we come across a new person, who is yet to pledge or give us goodie, he/she is approached with the list.

"Uncle Mike, compliment of the season, please promise me" Omonigho, who initially wasn't keen and involved, has now taken it more seriously than all of us immediately she became involved.

"What is promise me" Inquired Uncle Mike

And the list was thrust to him to peruse and tick any item listed.

"Ah, bicycle, water colors, crayons, chocolate, ball, sweets, money hmmmmm, ok take #500, I think I have tried", dipping his hand into his pocket to bring out the money and handing it over o Omonigho.

"Uncle thank you, God bless you" Omonigho obviously very happy after collecting the money said.

"Let's see how many items on your list got ticked" I inquired

We all compared notes and discovered that Omonigho made more money and her list got the highest ticks.
"Shebi, you were initially skeptical? I teased her
"Well that was before, I wish we can be doing this everyday and new year holiday will be everyday" She joyfully replied.
"Hmmmm, it can't be everyday oh" Felicia replied her.
"I know" Omonigho answered.
I left them and went to meet up with my friends, and we were just milling around the street all day only rushing home to have lunch and afterwards dinner, with some of them accompanying me home to join in the meal.
"It is almost time for watch night service, hope you guys won't stay out too late" Inquired my father.
'No sir".
"Okay, you guys take care of yourselves".
Himself, my mum, grand dad, grand mum and my siblings usually go to church together, I eventually will join them and being it was watch night service and new year's eve, the rules is very relaxed.
By this time myself, lukman and tunde have made up and are back being friends. Although muslims, they always follow us and the other guys for watch night service.
 By the time we got to church, the inside is already filled to the brim, necessitating our staying outside in the overflow which was exactly where we want to be.
With our pockets filled with bangers, knock-outs and fire crackers, our only interest is to hear the homily being said by Father Mathew "Now may the peace of our Lord Jesus Christ be upon you all and HAPPY NEW YEAR".

The bustle and bubble and shouts, with greetings of Happy New Year, followed with handshakes, hugs and of course our signal to unleash our arsenals.

Immediately fire crackers from different directions, fills the air and skies; boom boom can be heard everywhere.

Packing into the street afterward to continue with firing of knock-outs and fire crackers, as we make our way home.

It is a battle royale, even though due to security concerns, the State government through the police commissioner had banned firing of knock-outs, nonetheless this never deems the enthusiasm and excitement of indulging fully in it.

Due to blowing knock out almost all night, on getting home, my folks are already back and music is playing from the sitting room stereo, with the compound filled and brimming with activities. By early morning, the butchers who will slaughter the ram will arrive, after offertory and prayers has been made by Baba.

Sleep eventually overcame me but it was as if I had hardly slept before my tormentor-in- chief, Omonigho came shaking me to inform me that the ram has been slaughtered and am expected to go wash the entrails for use later as pepper soup.

Excitedly, I jumped up to my feet and left the room. "Good Morning Sir, good morning Ma, Aunty good morning, Uncle good morning and Happy New Year', I greeted everyone.

Seeing Baba sitting on the bench in front of the house, I approached cautiously, as I greeted him and wished him Happy New Year.

"Ah, Happy New Year and make sure, no troubles from you in this new year", He said with a cunning look on his face.

"No Sir, not at all Baba", I replied and ran away to where the bowl of intestines was to begin cleaning and removing the feaces and waste from its inside, while salivating in my mind the pepper soup that will follow later on before pounded yam and ogbono soup and black soup (whichever soup one chooses) afterwards.

I sure love this time of the year. HAPPY NEW YEAR.

107
SING MY SONG NOW

Sing for me now in my presence

And not later behind me in pretence

When it will have been a past tense.

I rather to be a living that is sung

Than a living that is unsung

Only to be a dead and be sung.

Should my going be

Caused by force majure

Then I absolve myself in the great ray.

Should my going not be

Caused by force majure

I remain restless until all are perjure.

Dedicated to Maj Gen Attahiru Jega and all those who lost their lives in the ill fated plane crash of 22nd May 2021.

108.
WETIN DEY INSIDE SEF

Wetin dey inside sef?

Wen dem dey stressing me

Just cos I wan blow!

Abegi ....

Wetin dey inside sef?

Abi no be relaxant e b again

For take coolu body?

I dunno....

Wetin dey inside sef?

No be to mix pleasure sweat

For make body be aiit?

E choke u…….

Wetin dey inside sef?

No be marathon

Na mostly sweet short distance.

Mad ooooo…..

I tell you

Wetin dey inside

Go take you to heaven come back.

Ball eeeee luyah…..

(wetin dey inside is a vernacular rendition meaning what's inside).

109
NO COMPETITION

You dey drive high lander

While I dey drive out lander.

Na same road we dey ply.

No competition.

You dey use IPhone 7

I dey use Itel 2.7

Na same browsing and calling we dey do

No competition

You get your kind girls you dey carry

I get me kind girls I dey carry

At the end na companion dem all be.

No competition.

You sabi chop for bistro

While me na iya oyo with her big stool.

Na belle we wan fiil.

No competition

You dey stay uptown

I dey stay downtown

All na make roof cover for head.

No competition.

Yu enter vip

While I dey general p

 Na same club we enter.

No competition

You order ten Hennessey for vip

I order one Hennessey for general p

Na same liquor we don drink.

No competition.

110
Poetry is.....

Poetry is community
community is poetry
The collective feeling
Put together in words
In rhythm, in rhyme

Poetry is individual
Individual is poetry

Communicating are felt
deep down from inner most part
Say it the way you feel it
Feel it the way you say it.

Poetry is life
Life is poetry
Observation, experience,
Penned down, and ribbed through written words.

111
Battleground NDA

We train from dusk till dawn.

Tama one a gruesome experience.

Tama two trench down exposure.

Tama three battle station so sure.

Tama four only eyes on tama five.

Tama five only eyes on passing out.

The battlefield seem far away.

Liberia, Sierra Leone, Bama, Sambisa.

Shots fired, shots fired, caught in their pants.

Only now at academy doorstep.

Training proving insufficients.

Officers rank and uniform demystified.

Battle lost even before started.

Rehabilitated infiltration on a mission.

Ransom now negotiated.

Under a country ran by a general captured.

(112)
LETTING LOOSE
My adrelanine is on hold...
waiting for the moment....
the right time to be free from its table...
conquering territories his sole ambition....
with itching hoofs and brewing fire nostrils....
temperature on the rising....
timing anchored on faith....
volcano erupting...
manifest restoration evolving....
more than a conqueror declaring....

BOOKS WRITTEN BY THE AUTHOR
STEPHEN O.I. ORUKPE ESQ.

 **THE ABC OF BUSINESS STUDIES I**

 **THE ABC OF BUSINESS STUDIES II**

 **THE ABC OF BUSINESS STUDIES III**

 **I HAVE A DREAM THAT ONE DAY WHEN I GROW UP I WILL BECOME...**

 **SOJOURNER METAMORPHOSIS (URBAN NOMAD)**

 **UNDERSTANDING THE INNER WORKINGS OF NIGERIA LEGISLATURE ECOWAS PARLIAMENT**

 **UNDERSTANDING, RUNNING AND CREATING WEALTH WITH COOPERATIVE SOCIETY**

 **THE STAYING POWER OF FOCUS**

 **INTERLOCUTORY APPLICATION**

 **UNDERSTANDING AND BEING SUCCESSFUL WITH NON PROFIT ORGANISATION (NGO) AND SUSTAINABLE DEVELOPMEN GOALS (SDGS)**

 **THE PEDESTRAIN**

 **DEMYSTIFYING THE ART OF EXAMINATION IN CHIEF, CROSS EXAMINATION, RE-EXAMINATIO ORAL, DOCUMENTARY AND ELECTRONIC EVIDENCE**

THE ABC OF BEING
YOUR OWN CEO

OILWELLS IN
OUR BACKYARD

WE MUST MOVE FORWARD
ABEG MAKE YOU NO VEX

www.ingramcontent.com/pod-product-compliance
Lightning Source LLC
LaVergne TN
LVHW061546070526
838199LV00077B/6927